DAVID

Man of Prayer,
Man of War

DAVID

Man of Prayer, Man of War

Walter J. Chantry

THE BANNER OF TRUTH TRUST

THE BANNER OF TRUTH TRUST
3 Murrayfield Road, Edinburgh EH12 6EL
P.O. Box 621, Carlisle, PA 17013, USA

ISBN-13: 978 0 85151 953 1

Typeset in 11/14 pt Bembo at the
Banner of Truth Trust, Edinburgh

Printed in the U.S.A. by
Versa Press, Inc.,
East Peoria, IL

CONTENTS

INTRODUCTION

Only the supreme providence of God and the unfathomable depths of divine grace could have conceived and forged the life of David. God made the son of Jesse into the emblem of the kingly office which only Christ would fulfil more gloriously. He embodied all the qualities of manly nobility and charm. Everyone in his day loved David, except the most ugly and despicable figures. It is just the same for those in our day who hear the history of *Samuel*[1] and *Chronicles* being read.

David lived through the most diverse conditions of human experience, and this alone calls forth our deepest feelings of sympathy. For a time he enjoyed the solitude of a pastoral scene. Yet, suddenly he was transported to the royal court and called into service as a balladeer.

This in turn was only a stepping-stone to his becoming the champion of the armies of Israel, the subject of young women's songs and old men's toasts.

The truth is that David never settled into one niche for long. Soon after being heralded as a hero, the young man became a hunted refugee, a dashing figure as he led a band of outlaws in the deserts. Again with suddenness David

[1] *Samuel:* 1 & 2 Samuel appear as one book in the Hebrew Old Testament.

became king of Judah and a few years later of Israel as well. He vanquished all of his and his people's foes, establishing a kingdom that would last for four hundred years. But no sooner was this accomplished than he was plunged into a foul sin, even though he had arrived at a mature age. Never again would he have peace. Thenceforth his family life proved to be filled with rebellion and murder.

The one constant with David in every condition was expressed in Psalm 16:8: 'I have set the LORD *always* before me.'

In all the rapid alterations of his life David thought of the Most High God and expressed his devout feelings toward his Maker and Redeemer. When he wept in shame for his loathsome sins, his tears were poured out before the Lord. When he felt the exhilaration of triumph, he shouted to the Lord who was his strength.

Perhaps this most of all explains the vast variety of David's life experiences. The Lord made him into the Psalmist for all the saints in all subsequent ages. In his youth he knew a peaceful, tranquil walk with God; in later years he both walked upon the heights and fell into the depths, and thus was enabled to compose prayerful songs for every condition of life.

No matter how high David rose above other men, his spirit was childlike toward the Lord. Therefore he did not make pretentious efforts of self-defence with others. His sorrow in confession was immediately and deeply expressed without any consideration for who might be watching. He who was equally at home holding the shepherd's staff, the warrior's sword, the poet's harp, and the ruler's sceptre, was completely transparent in the humbling of himself before the God of all the earth. This ease and simplicity in worship draws out our deepest emotions as we read the life of David, King of Israel. We love this man for showing us how to pray from every point of life's compass. We love him for showing us how, in the midst of spiritual failure, we too can draw near to the Lord again in trust and devotion.

Perfectionists will not be comfortable with David. Those who stumble often, but who always turn with melted hearts to God for pardon and help, will find in him a brother for all situations. Such people will love the sacred history of his life and find it totally engrossing.

WALTER J. CHANTRY
February 2007

I

A MAN AFTER GOD'S OWN HEART

1 Samuel 15:34–16:1

A heart–melting scene is described for us in this passage. An aging prophet of outstanding spiritual stature and service is disconsolate. He is immobilized with grief for and fear of an associate in God's service who has now turned quite mad.

This weeping prophet was named Samuel. When his story is all told, it will be clear that he was God's instrument to turn round the spiritual fortunes of Israel at a most dark hour. But at that moment his efforts seemed to be turned into a shambles and he trembled for the people of God. The hope with which he had ministered now seemed to him an unreachable dream.

Samuel laboured during the midnight blackness and early dawn of two eras in Israel. God always preserves his people. Christ always builds his church. When Joshua and the elders who served with him died, Israel as a nation began many cycles of spiritual decline. There were intermittent revivals of true religion only to be followed by Israel's making a further descent. This period continued for centuries, until Samuel was born.

The now-famous boy-prophet had, as his first commission, to pronounce God's curse on the priests at Shiloh. On that spot the tabernacle had been settled after the war of conquest. In keeping with Samuel's curse, the priests were chased off to Nob, Eli's home, the sanctuary was destroyed by Philistines, and even, for a time, the ark of the covenant was in enemy hands. Shiloh, the national place of religious pilgrimage, where Samuel had spent his earliest years, became a mark of God's wrathful scourge. Samuel carried out his adult ministry from Ramah, a town near the ruins of Shiloh. It is at Ramah that we find the prophet in momentary depression.

Through Samuel's vigorous prophetic ministry, there were true religious stirrings throughout the nation. There was even spectacular military victory over the Philistines under his national leadership. He had lived through the crisis of having had God's people ask for a king because they distrusted God. He had anointed Saul as the first king of Israel.

The Benjamite king seemed to begin well. Samuel, under God's direction, forged a new task for prophets. He began the work of providing a check and balance to the nearly-autocratic monarchs of Israel. God's spokesmen would have access to the rulers of Israel to deliver the will and word of God for the nation. Samuel entered into a relationship in which he spoke to the king as no other mere mortal would have dared. With boldness and plainness he instructed, commanded, and rebuked the king, when he had a word from God. For a time, it seemed that Saul feared God and his prophet.

Then there came a series of disastrous acts of disobedience by Saul, followed by confrontations of the king by Samuel. These confrontations were most unpleasant for Saul and for Samuel. The work of discipline is never pleasant to ministers. God's servants' hearts are broken when they observe that disobedience is hardening into a pattern despite faithful opposition to it. No wonder Samuel was beset with a woeful spirit.

The Lord gently rebuked Samuel while he was overwhelmed with grief for Saul, for Israel, and for the outcome of his ministry. 'How long will you grieve?' There follows a series of commands to be active again. The work of this man of God is not finished. He will yet preside spiritually over brighter days.

Even before the rejection of Saul as king occurred, God had spoken to Saul (or was it especially to Samuel?) words of encouragement for Israel that were intertwined with those of doom for Saul. In 1 Samuel 13 came the brightest promise, giving threads of hope in the midst of condemnation.

Is that not a pattern with the Almighty? When men make a thorough shambles of obeying God's commands, he comes to them to announce his just curses, but in doing so he drops the brightest jewels of promise. It was that way in Genesis 3 after Adam and Eve had sinned, spoiled paradise, and plunged the human race into a legacy of sin and misery. There we have the first promise of Christ (*Gen.* 3:15).

In 1 Samuel 13, Israel was invaded by the Philistines again. The entire nation was in a panic at the threat of this enemy. Samuel gave Saul explicit instructions from the Lord. Saul disobeyed by offering sacrifices to God. Samuel told Saul that, had he been obedient to the word of God, 'The LORD would have established your kingdom over Israel forever. But now your kingdom shall not continue. The LORD has sought out a man after his own heart, and the LORD has commanded him to be prince over his people, because you have not kept what the LORD commanded you' (*1 Sam.* 13:13–14). What a dramatic moment!

There is 'a man after God's own heart'. The Lord had looked for him and had found him. He will rule instead of Saul. Here is no good news for Saul, but it is great news for Samuel and for Israel. From the context it is clear that 'a man after God's own heart' refers to a man who has an inclination to obey the Lord. Psalm 89:20 records the Lord as having said, 'I have found David, my servant; with my holy oil I have anointed him.' Many years later, the Apostle Paul preached in Antioch that, when God had removed Saul, 'he raised up David to be their king, of whom he testified and said, "I have found in David the son of Jesse a man after my heart, who will do all my will"' (*Acts* 13:22).

Today the Lord continues to search for men after his own heart to lead his people, his churches. That which he longs to find is a steadfastness in obeying his commands. Saul found himself in desperate crises in which something had to be done quickly. He was under multiple pressures from enemies and friends, which demanded that decisions be taken. In these moments of confusion he disobeyed God's clear word of direction.

The not-yet-disclosed 'man after God's own heart' would, in coming years, face no less urgent and perilous events. He would be under the strains of conflicting counsel from within and without. Yet he would choose to obey the Lord's directives in emergencies, even when it was not clear to him how his obedience would resolve pressing difficulties. How this man would bow to the word of the Lord by Nathan the prophet in the most entangled of circumstances was to be a refreshing scene.

When church officers are brought to immobility in solving a church deadlock, are there no clear commands to be obeyed in the circumstances? It may seem that these acts of obedience could not untie the knots of difficulty. However, God may arise to deliver when his servants follow his words.

All the arguments which seem rational in the tangles of testing – 'It will only deepen the conflict'; 'It will create more tension and strife'; 'It will accomplish nothing' – may only reveal unbelieving hearts. Where is the man who will simply do what the Lord has said? He who is 'after my heart' 'will do all my will'.

Saul's hardened heart displayed foolishness from which his subordinates were forced to restrain him. Then the Lord sent Saul to destroy the Amalekites. Again, explicit instructions were given. Again, the king of Israel disobeyed. Samuel now accused him of rebellion against the Lord, a crime quite as grim as witchcraft (in which Saul would dabble in the future). Thus Samuel announced, 'The LORD. . . has also rejected you from being king' (*1 Sam.* 15:23).

Where can one find such bold confrontations of rulers, but in Scripture?

After this sensational face-off, Samuel turned to go. The king seized the prophet's robe and tore it. Samuel then said, 'The LORD has torn the kingdom of Israel from you this day and has given it to a neighbour of yours, who is better than you' (*1 Sam.* 15:28). Here is another nugget of golden hope!

However, we are breathless to see such electrifying boldness in Samuel. He has insisted on the supremacy of God's word over kings! It was the very last time Samuel would see Saul in this world. Saul was no longer Samuel's chosen king, as he was no longer God's.

Samuel is nonetheless despondent. He had liked Saul. He had placed hope in his reign. He had poured his heart and soul into assisting and recovering Saul. Now what prospect was there? His own lips had spoken of 'a man after God's own heart', of the kingdom of Israel being 'given to a neighbour of yours, who is better than you'. Therefore, the Lord told Samuel that he must not be incapacitated by grief for past disappointments. 'Fill your horn with oil, and go. I will send you to Jesse the Bethlehemite, for I have provided for myself a king among his sons' (*1 Sam.* 16:1). The Lord has sought and found 'a man after his own heart', who will do all his will. The word of God will be this man's law. 'A king among Jesse's sons', says God, but what is his name?

Most names are forgotten within a few years of their owners' deaths. A few are remembered for a millennium. Fewer still of these are recalled with admiration. The New Testament begins with these words: 'The book of the genealogy of Jesus Christ, the son of David, the son of Abraham' (*Matt.* 1:1).

Three names will stand above most others forever. The first has a rank of its own, for Jesus Christ is David's Lord as well as David's son (*Matt.* 22:43–45). David's first connection to Jesus Christ as servant has much more to do with his fragrant remembrance than with his having been an ancestor of the Messiah. Jesus' name is above all others. He is Lord over all. It is those who bow to him who will be known as the righteous ones.

The Most High God spoke to the great prophet Samuel about David before ever the young man's name was given to Samuel. David was living in a small village called Bethlehem. He was accounted least of all by members of the family in which he lived. Even at the most important social and religious events, his absence was considered reasonable. He would be sent into the fields to tend sheep, while the remainder of the family attended to matters of greater consequence.

David was with the animals in the pasture as great international events engaged armies of his nation. Spiritual forces were at work in the land. The Almighty, who brings princes to nothing, was doing just that, while the teenager continued to husband the livestock. Samuel, the greatest living spiritual figure in Israel was sent to the house of Jesse to anoint a new king. Until God named his choice in Samuel's ear, no one thought God was seeking the lad with the blush of field-life on his cheeks. Others had nobler appearances and more promise, in human judgment.

A boy working with a flock seems isolated from great events of history. But he is the link between the past and the future of the kingdom of God; even in his obscure condition, he was 'a man after God's own heart'. His name is David! He will put obedience to God's word above sacrifice and hearkening to his prophets above the fat of rams.

Are there not young men who even now have the Almighty's eye upon them? They cannot yet wear the armour of the warrior, nor find their way through the labyrinth of king's courts or church boards. The Lord looks not for experience; that is easily given. He wishes to detect, deep within the character of youth, submission to all the will of God.

2

THE LORD LOOKS ON THE HEART

1 Samuel 16:2–14

'The LORD looks on the heart' (*1 Sam.* 16:7). God had seen that David already was 'a man after his own heart' (*1 Sam.* 13:14). But Samuel's first glimpse (and ours) of this fascinating figure of history comes on the day of David's anointing.

He would become the champion of armies, a fugitive in the desert, living as a sort of 'Robin Hood' to the people of God, while pursued by a mad man. He would sit on the throne of Israel, leading God's people to a golden era. He would oversee a new administration of the covenant of grace, instituting new patterns of worship and personally writing the greatest prayer book of all time. He would be a prodigal, falling deeply into sin, but humbly blazing a trail of repentance to give all sinners hope. How many facets there would be to David's life!

Yet, as he had a horn of oil poured on his head, he was a simple teen-aged shepherd in a small agricultural village.

1. The record of David's anointing reminds us that human authorities strike fear into the hearts of their fellow men.

Samuel spent some time when he was not reconciled to the secret purposes of God through which he had passed. Personal attachments to Saul and anxiety for the future of Israel brought the prophet into a grieving state of inertia.

A gentle rebuke from the Lord and the surprising announcement that there was another king to anoint awakened the man of God into a state of fear.

Yes, Samuel had boldly withstood the king to his face in the name of the Lord. But then, men of God often find courage to speak in the power of the Spirit which is not native to their own frames. Saul was already under the power of an evil spirit. He would have unjustly slain his very own son, had not others restrained him. What would this king, abusive of authority from God, do to Samuel if he anointed a rival for Saul's own throne? In Eastern lands, from time immemorial, regimes had changed only by civil war or the most bloody mutinies. In terror, this brave servant of God said to the Lord, 'If Saul hears of it, he will kill me!'

Samuel was directed to Bethlehem with plans to hide his mission from Saul. As he travelled along the way, leading a heifer for sacrifice, he would surely have known that Rachel was buried at Bethlehem. Had he also heard the beautiful account of David's great-grandfather, Boaz, and his great-grandmother, Ruth? Did he think of these events along the way? Did it occur to him that these events were to be related to the Messiah?

As Samuel arrived in Bethlehem, there was a scene many ministers of the gospel have shared. The man of God was greeted by trembling elders of the town, asking, 'Do you come peaceably?' God sometimes told a prophet who received revelations the sins of individuals and communities so that he might rebuke them, call them to repentance or pronounce curses on the hard of heart. Had Samuel's last mission not been a stormy pronouncement of doom on a king?

Ministers must realize that their people have trembled under the Word of God which they preach. Consciences have been exposed under preaching in such dramatic ways that sinners flee from the church, wondering who has told the minister about them.

All of us have seen the fear in the eyes of congregation members until they are assured by us that our present visit is for peaceful purposes. Never must a minister abuse this part of his calling to tease or to terrify for personal reasons. Rebukes must be used only for serious sins of the impenitent.

2. The record of David's anointing carries a most instructive word from the Lord.

Samuel obediently went to the house of Jesse to make it plain that he had a special desire for Jesse and his sons to attend the sacrifice. What an honour it was to have such exceptional attention from this prophet, so legendary to all in the nation!

As Jesse and his seven sons prepared for the feast, Samuel was impressed by Eliab, the eldest son. No doubt he was tall, mature, well educated, ready, even then, to march into battle with Saul. Samuel thought, 'Surely the LORD's anointed is before him.'

We all have our plans for God's kingdom, our assessments of those most suited for leadership among God's people. The Lord spoke to Samuel in these memorable words, 'Do not look on his appearance or on the height of his stature, because I have rejected him. For the LORD sees not as man sees: man looks on the outward appearance, but the LORD looks on the heart.' Here was a great spiritual man at full maturity and with long experience in God's kingdom on earth. Yet Samuel still evaluated by observing the outward appearance. Man always does that. Only God 'looks at the heart'.

This is true even in our self-evaluations. To some extent, I can look into my own heart as God can. No other man may do so. God and I have access to the inner workings of my heart (mind, emotions, will). However, as Jeremiah 17:9–10 tells us, 'The heart is deceitful above all things, and desperately sick; who can understand it? I the LORD search the heart and test the mind.' There are depths to our sin which are self-deceiving.

Too many imagine that a democratic method of choosing church officers is the safest. But in the New Testament, apostles searched the Scriptures for qualifications, prayed and fasted to know the will of the God who 'looks on the heart'. Do our churches still fast and pray to have ministers, elders, and deacons who are 'after God's own heart'? Or have we grown content with constitutions and 'Book of Order' processes?

When we look at other men and seek to judge their spirituality or sincerity of character, let us never forget this text. Perhaps churches are shocked by seeing apostates go out from their midst as periodic reminders that man is always observing outward appearances and that only the Lord searches hearts. Those who vainly imagine they have a gift for discerning the condition of others' hearts are due to receive serious disappointments.

Thus every group of elders who rightly judge the profession of faith and experience of those who wish to be church members must remember that they do not look upon hearts. They examine credible professions and outward evidences only. Over the years, spiritually minded elders will find that they have been too doubtful about some and too confident about others who join their churches.

Samuel, at the height of his service to God, is humbled by his inability to judge Jesse's sons. Had he seen Eliab in the Valley of Elah, serving in Saul's army, he would never have said, 'Surely the LORD's anointed is before him.' None of the seven was the 'man after God's own heart'. So Jesse summoned his eighth son. Finally David stood before Samuel. He was handsome, but so were Jesse's other sons. Samuel anointed David for only one reason. 'And the LORD said, "Arise, anoint him, for this is he."'

It was the Lord who chose David to be king, not Samuel nor the people of Israel. Nothing that we can observe was decisive with God. He chose David for the unseen qualities of the inner man. God finds his servants in unexpected places: Joseph in a prison, David in a sheep pen, Luther in a miner's cottage. At the lowest point of his life, David was to cry, 'Behold, you delight in truth in the inward being, and you teach me wisdom in the secret heart' (*Psa.* 51:6). In Psalm 66:18 the Psalmist of Israel wrote, 'If I had cherished iniquity in my heart, the Lord would not have listened.' David's son by Bathsheba wrote, 'Keep your heart with all vigilance, for from it flow the springs of life' (*Prov.* 4:23). The Lord searches your heart. What does he find?

3. The anointing of David was attended with spiritual realities.

God commands that symbols and ceremonies be used. Samuel was told to anoint the lad with oil. It was an act rich with meaning. But God himself gave the reality! 'And the Spirit of the LORD rushed upon David from that day forward.'

At that hour, the youth of Jesse's house entered a new phase of development for his inner life. For the most part, David will keep in step with the Spirit. He would not be conscious of the Spirit stirring within him at every moment. At times he would be profoundly aware that he was unlike any other man, because he was full of the Spirit. He would grow to cherish the inward operations of the Spirit. After his fall into adultery and murder, he would give his anguished cry, 'Cast me not away from your presence, and take not your Holy Spirit from me' (*Psa.* 51:11).

Immediately after seeing that the Spirit had fallen upon David, we are told, 'Now the Spirit of the LORD departed from Saul.' David personally observed the piteous and horrific consequences of the Spirit of God having left a man so as to lend no more of his operations to that person's life.

Do you treasure the Holy Spirit as a guest in your heart? Do you labour not to grieve the Spirit, not to quench the Spirit? When you sin, do you anxiously pray, 'Take not your Holy Spirit from me'? He is the Spirit of truth, the Spirit of life, the Spirit of peace and joy. He is the Spirit of righteousness, the Spirit of worship, the Spirit by whom we commune with the Father and the Son. He is the Spirit of power and of grace. We stand amazed at the life of David. Here is the explanation of all that was to follow: 'The Spirit of the LORD rushed upon David.'

'If you then, who are evil, know how to give good gifts to your children, how much more will the heavenly Father give the Holy Spirit to those who ask him!' (Jesus, in *Luke* 11:13). Is this on your prayer list? Can it be found amidst your desires for health, safety, and prosperity? Do you pray more for leaders than for the Spirit?

In our Christian assemblies, may we have less of appearances, less of empty ceremony, and more of the Spirit attending biblical forms.

3

THE LORD IS WITH HIM

1 Samuel 16:14–23

'Behold, I have seen a son of Jesse the Bethlehemite . . . and the LORD is with him (*1 Sam.* 16:18).

We learn from 1 Samuel 16:14–23 that the stealthy measures used by the aging prophet Samuel succeeded. The anointing of David remained unknown to Saul. Keeping the king ignorant of a rival was a required part of God's plan to prepare a teenage shepherd to become ruler of his people.

Divine providence arranged for David to have immediate experience with powerful spiritual realities and to make first-hand observations of a king's court. There the youth would have objective views of flattery, deceit, pretence, hypocrisy, and intrigue by rogues, and faithful counsel and loyal service by the humble of heart.

Justice from the Almighty provided a need for David's services. 'An evil spirit from the LORD tormented him', troubled Saul (*1 Sam.* 16:14). The king's spirit was overcome with a dark spiritual cloud of paranoia, tormenting irrational suspicion, and terror. These impressions made by an evil spirit drove him to impetuous, violent rage. They also twisted his personality into irreconcilable, intermittent emotions of passionate hatred and fatuous tenderness toward the same person. All of this madness was provoked by an evil spirit.

Providence arranged that wise and bold counsellors attend Saul in his demented state. With simple directness they told the king, 'Behold now, an evil spirit from God is tormenting you.'

His servants knew that rulers in such a condition could find relief from their feverish agonies of spirit by means of music. Providence had also arranged that someone at court had met David, the shepherd lad, had heard his extraordinary musical skills and was in a position to suggest David's services just at the moment when Saul accepted his counsellors' advice.

Imagine the teenager's frame of mind when he was summoned to Saul's home (there was, as yet, no palace or national capital)! Trusted advisors of the monarch would tell the inexperienced young man that the king was tormented by a demon. When the ruler's spirit was most agitated and madness reigned over his countenance, words and actions, other servants would flee the room and the young shepherd would be sent in to play his harp. More than once, as David sought to calm his master's spirit, he would have to dodge the thrust of the crazed warrior's spear.

What teen today would like to take such an internship? In this portion of Scripture a view of reality is expressed to which Western society has largely turned a blind eye. Unashamedly the Bible emphasizes the existence of spiritual reality! This world cannot be understood unless attention is given to the existence and mighty influence of spirits. By definition spirits are non-material. Therefore, those who judge reality by empirical proofs only have, by their choice of epistemology, shut their eyes to a most significant aspect of true being. Science, devoted exclusively to empirical observation, has nothing whatever to contribute on the vast subject of the spiritual.

Foremost in the text is God. As Jesus said, when he was on earth, 'God is spirit' (*John* 4:24). There is no material aspect to him. Or, as a child's catechism teaches, 'God is a Spirit and has not a body like men.' As Genesis 1:1 states, 'In the beginning God created the heavens and the earth.' God (the Supreme Spirit) is before all, above all, and behind all. Creation is the act of an eternal, self-existent Spirit, bringing into existence all lesser spirits and all material reality. This involves a spiritual cause of material effects. It is absurd to speak of science investigating such a proposition; for science investigates only material cause and effect. It is 'by faith we understand that the universe was created by the word of God . . .' (*Heb.* 11:3).

It is not by scientific proof or investigation that such conclusions are reached. Many great scientists have faith, and thereby detect the glory of God in their studies of his creation. However it is not by sensual observations alone that they reach these conclusions. Mixed with their empirical data are spiritual perceptions. Man has powers of spiritual cognition as well as those of sensual perception. Spiritual awareness is informed and increased by divine revelation, that is, by the Word of God.

Furthermore, when God, the Almighty Spirit, created all things, he continued to rule, direct, and administer all the affairs of heaven and earth. There is direct influence by a Spiritual Being upon all material creation, in matters great and small, at every instant. Ignoring this spiritual influence and power dooms observers to darkness of understanding.

Saul's counsellors did not ignore God's direct involvement in Saul's madness, nor the influence of a lesser and evil spirit. Therefore, they were wise and full of understanding. As another ruler, driven into temporary madness, commented after being relieved of his dementia, 'The Most High . . . does according to his will among the host of heaven and among the inhabitants of the earth' (*Dan.* 4:34–35). He further adds that no one can restrain his hand (as a parent might do when correcting a child), or ask him, 'What have you done?'

Spiritual powers, good and evil, are very much present at the seats of national power. David must have a close-up view of spiritual forces, both good and evil. He will one day be in the midst of conflicts involving principalities, powers, and spiritual rulers in heavenly places.

Even as a youth, 'The Spirit of the LORD rushed upon him.' Even as a youth, he looked into the crazed eye of Saul, possessed of an evil spirit. Although greater was he that was in David than he that was in Saul, and although

God delivered David from a madman and a devil, yet David could not cast out the evil spirit.

He might become king, but he would learn his limitations and his dependence on the Almighty Spirit. The dispositions and moods of human spirits are not influenced only by social and material environments; they are acted upon by divine and demonic spirits. Thus all who labour to soothe the troubled spirits of men must be humbled. At times they are involved with spiritual powers not wholly subject to counselling, scientific analysis, or chemical manipulation.

The Lord sends his Holy Spirit to some and evil spirits to others. No spirit is subject to human processes but by the grace of God. Musical therapy for oppressed minds is not a modern discovery. There are sacred and secular records of this treatment dating from ancient times. Human spirits may be improved greatly by the use of appropriate music. The positive effect may only be temporary, but it may utterly reverse the influence of evil spirits upon a man's soul. How many are prescribing music for tormented minds in our day? 'And whenever the evil spirit from God was upon Saul, David took the lyre and played it with his hand. So Saul was refreshed and was well, and the evil spirit departed from him' (*1 Sam.* 16:23).

When we read such an account, it is impossible to imagine that all music is neutral and that only the words of songs have positive or negative impact. We are not told that David sang to Saul but that he used instrumental music for his spiritual wellbeing. Have you not heard some music designed to inflame passions, create agitation, foment rebellion, and even create fear? A man having the Spirit of the Lord (which Spirit brings righteousness and peace and joy; see *Rom.* 14:17), plays for a man having an evil spirit (which spirit produces anger, murder, tumult, and fear).

This music, influenced by the Spirit of the Lord, drives away the evil spirit. The music itself is not neutral! Is it impossible for those who are made wise by God's Word to judge the spirits in music? How did David know what tunes to play? How will you know what tunes will soothe the troubled hearts of the saints in worship?

What a change of scenery for David! Taken from the quiet country meadows and streams, he was introduced into a world of evil spirits and deranged humanity. But his future prayer book must have compositions concerning those who face sinister enemies, both human and demonic. Prayers must be composed for those who fight against foes which mean to destroy them. Prayers must be made for all who stand in positions of power and dominion.

David, in his new school, discovered that the judgments of God are fearful. 'It is a fearful thing to fall into the hands of the living God' (*Heb.* 10:31). Gone forever are cheerful and hopeful days for Saul. David observed a man of influence and wealth. As David's father sent a present to the king, so no man appeared before an eastern monarch without some gift. Yet this king's disposition was debased and bitter.

Saul would never be what he wished he could be. He was shut up in a prison of depression, deserted by God. A very young David was called to stand beside a gruesome specimen of depraved and twisted humanity. Saul was wounded in spirit to the depths, a miserable man, broken and lost! It is possible to sin away opportunities for recovery. Oh, the brooding gloom of those whose souls are hardened and whose doom is sealed while yet alive! Did not this lasting impression incite the writing of Psalm 51 in David's most prodigal hour? When he held the reins of state in his mature years and could commit adultery and murder without fear of human reprisals, he shuddered with the fear of God. His steps were so near to those of the hopeless mad man to whom he had ministered in his youth that his prayer to God was all the more urgent.

But God's judgments for sin are sure. Does not Revelation 20 speak of a lake of fire, into which the devil is cast, as the place to which the impenitent are consigned? Some have joked that there will be a happy society in hell. The actual effect of evil spirits upon the human spirit is depicted by Saul. To dwell in such company of evil spirits forever will be an unbearable torment. Thither go the Cains and Sauls and Judases of this world. These who are driven to wild and frenzied acts of violence against others and themselves have evil spirits influencing them. We think of the appalling refrain of Romans 1:24, 26, and 28, 'Therefore God gave them up.'

However powerful the influences of evil are upon you, 'Seek the LORD while he may be found; call upon him while he is near' (*Isa.* 55:6). When Jesus was on earth, he not only drove evil spirits out of men temporarily, as did David by music; he *commanded* demons to exit men permanently by his word. He filled men with his Spirit so that there was no room for the evil spirits to move back in. These demons trembled before Jesus and cried out in terror of him. He is able to save to the uttermost those who draw near to God through him.

Go to God by Jesus, however lost and broken and twisted your humanity. No minister or counsellor or musician can do for you all that you need.

> None but Jesus, none but Jesus
> Can do helpless sinners good.

He is at God's right hand. Approach him with your heart by prayer. You must personally seek his aid. 'Jesus, Son of David, have mercy on me!' (*Luke* 18:38). Heaven will be forever populated by those who pray such prayers from their hearts. Some will be rescued from a condition very near to that of Saul. Who can tell if you will be one of them? Seek Christ at once!

The highest commendation given to David, when Saul's servants suggested employing him, was, 'The LORD is with him.' Accounts of David are used to describe the servants with whom the Lord is pleased to dwell. They are men who have a disposition after God's own heart, an inclination to obey him.

This is found by the eye of God which scrutinizes the innermost recesses of the hearts of men. The Spirit of the Lord comes upon them. God is with them as they live. He walks with them. They are his people and he is their God. Their service is effective in frightful places of deepest darkness. It is because the Almighty is with them.

4

DAVID AND SAUL

1 Samuel 17:1–39

Throughout Western literature we meet the phrase, 'David and Goliath'! It looks back to the battlefield of two ancient combatants. So the phrase attaches itself to any conflict in which the little fellow beats the foe of enormous strength. Yet in Scripture the historic event might well be called 'David and Saul'. 1 Samuel 16:13–14 has told us, 'And the Spirit of the LORD rushed upon David from that day forward . . . Now the Spirit of the LORD departed from Saul.' In the Valley of Elah, the significance of the Holy Spirit shines brightly through the contrast between David and Saul.

Neither man came to the Valley of Elah by a personal decision, or in following a subjective impulse given by God's Spirit. The Philistines, warlike inhabitants of Palestine's seacoast, marched a great army into Judah. (Invasions by them were perpetual.) Saul, with all his dark moods of irrational rage and depressions of regret, must summon his troops and face the irritating challenge. He was responsible for leading his army in defence of Israel. Will the Philistines never cease their hostilities? David, who had three brothers enlisted among Saul's conscripts, was sent by his father to bear gifts to his soldier-sons and to bring back word of their well-being. Fathers of every era are anxious about their sons at war. A family messenger was preferred above a letter.

David had ministered to demon-troubled Saul with music, but a bitter enmity toward David was now in the heart of Saul. Therefore, David had returned to shepherd duties in his father's household at Bethlehem. Now the two were to meet again. Saul approached the scene with reluctant necessity; David arrived in obedience to his father's will. Above them both was a divine providence placing David and Saul in counterpoise. God is showing us a man filled with the Spirit in bold relief against a man without the Spirit. Especially evident are the consequences for leadership in each case.

As David gave his brothers messages and gifts from home, and as he took information to be carried back to the homestead, the voice of a bellicose Philistine soldier pierced the air. A gigantic warrior, more than nine feet tall, a mountain of a man, carrying a huge sword and spear, was challenging any Israelite soldier to a personal duel, to one-on-one combat. Each would represent his entire army. The fate of the two armies would rest on this fight.

In the giant's speech was a tone of self-confident boasting, a note of mocking his foes, and a defiant blasphemy of their God. Philistia had a champion! A scornful ultimatum rang through the camp of Israel. Who will dare to face this Goliath?

David noted the demoralized response of Saul's army. 'They were dismayed and greatly afraid.' 'All the men of Israel, when they saw the man, fled from him and were much afraid.' For forty days Goliath cried out with insolence, with contempt for the Jewish army.

Meanwhile, the warrior-king of Israel stayed in his tent. He had no stomach for the battle. He made faint-hearted attempts to bribe someone in his ranks to accept the challenge. At first there was the offer of silver and gold; to this was added his daughter's hand in marriage. Then perpetual exemption from taxation was promised. The man whom the Spirit of God had left hoped to find a way of escape without personal commitment or risk of blood. His timidity insinuated itself through all the forces under his command.

1. God's Spirit Incites Zeal

David began to be agitated with the rising heat of zeal in his breast as he listened to the repeated insults of Goliath. Of his brothers and their fellow infantrymen the youngest son of Jesse began to ask, 'Who is this uncircumcised Philistine, that he should defy the armies of the living God?' He was stirred to the depths with concern for the glory of God. A mere creature defies the living God, while those who claim to fight in the cause of the Almighty are craven with fear! The honour of the Lord of hosts must be vindicated! The hot lava of zeal is erupting in his soul.

The man upon whom the Spirit has come is younger than everyone else at the Valley of Elah. But age and experience are not the issue. Clear vision of the unassailable grandeur of the Lord, brought into focus by the operations of the Holy Spirit, is the crux of the matter.

Does it not rouse you likewise, in our age, to hear blasphemies from fellow-workers and in college dormitories? Does no heat rise within you as you listen to atheistic professors defying the living God? Attacks on truth and righteousness—yes, more than that, on the Lord—are all around you! Young men, will you not take up the sword of the Spirit against God's enemies? Others, with miserable cowardice, hide in the bushes. Old men, grown cautious, hold back. Surely the Spirit will compel someone to volunteer: 'Your servant will go and fight with this Philistine.' 'It is good to be zealous in a good thing' (*Gal.* 4:18, NKJV). Many a man has his finest hour in his youth.

Saul had been drained of all enthusiasm to fight the Lord's battles. He has disobeyed the Lord repeatedly. There remains for him no assurance that the Lord goes with him. In Saul and David is fulfilled the proverb, 'The wicked flee when no one pursues, but the righteous are bold as a lion' (*Prov.* 28:1). Sin makes men into cowards. Obedience builds courage.

2. God's Spirit Incites Faith

For such a long time, Saul had been looking for someone to be the defender of Israel's cause against the giant. Therefore, David's words of indignation at the insults of the monster from Gath were reported to the king. As David repeated to Saul his offer to fight Goliath, the dispirited ruler expressed his doubts: 'You are not able to go against this Philistine to fight with him, for you are but a youth, and he has been a man of war from his youth.'

David had no résumé of experience to recommend him. He did not look the part of a warrior. The Philistine was every inch a man of war in appearance and in record of past victories. Saul's personal fears attached themselves to the young shepherd offering himself to fight. All was based on human logic and measurements of size and of history in past military encounters.

The young man filled with the Spirit had his confidence, not in personal prowess, but in what the Almighty would do to aid him. He did have a résumé of experience in receiving help from heaven. As a shepherd he had faced a lion. The beast of prey had seized a lamb of his father's flock for whose safety he was responsible. By faith in his God, he had seized the lion by its beard and clubbed it to death. On another occasion his victorious combat with a bear had been similar. 'The LORD who delivered me from the paw of the lion and from the paw of the bear will deliver me from the hand of this Philistine.' His undoubting reliance was upon a proven Lord. It was the unanswerable syllogism of faith.

3. God's Spirit Incites Wisdom

Far from being unbridled passion or unreasonable emotion, David's zealous faith was marked by admirable self-control. When David first openly expressed his annoyance at the gall of a heathen to insult the God of

Israel, Eliab, his eldest brother, angrily berated him. No doubt Eliab felt the sting of David's courage as a contrast to his own cowardice in the situation.

David would not be drawn into conflict with his brother, even though his character and motives had been assaulted. His indignation was against the enemy of God's people, not against a brother, however mistaken. Absorbing the insults, he modestly responded, 'What have I done now? Was it not but a word?' How often do our hearts enter upon a mission for God against his enemies, only to expend our emotional capital against carping brothers and sisters. The Spirit of wisdom restrained David from this error.

As David spoke with Saul, it must have been evident by facial expression and tone of voice that the general of the Lord's host was cringing as much as were his untested recruits. Yet, David speaks humbly of himself as Saul's servant. He addresses his king in reassuring terms.

Here is insight into David's wisdom, a wisdom that came from above. He had observed Saul under the dominion of an evil spirit as much as anyone had. Now he observed his deteriorating character which made him unable to take the initiative demanded by his office. Young men are apt, because of fallen human nature, to mock authorities with such obvious flaws. God's wisdom advises, 'My son, fear the LORD and the king' (*Prov.* 24:21). David honours his king.

How often Saul had relied on human strategies in disregard of the commands of the Lord! Again the sovereign of Israel thinks only of providing David with the armaments of great warriors. In submission the lad attempts to wear the armour provided by his acknowledged leader. But the youth recognizes what the aging king does not see. It is unavailing to wear what he finds restrictive or to fight with weapons he does not know how to wield.

The volunteer for the duel with Goliath prefers the staff, the sling, and the shepherd's pouch. His wisdom far surpasses that of the experienced soldier. Proven weapons and commonplace tactics in facing enemies are to be preferred to cumbersome defences and unfamiliar ways. The simplicity of wisdom from the Spirit of God is refreshing. In David it is humbly expressed.

How is it that some tell us the saints did not possess the Spirit in the Old Testament era? It is true that they did not possess the fullness of his revelation objectively given, nor did they have the fullness of the Spirit's inward operations upon the least in the kingdom of God, as would be given in the New Covenant. Yet, as we observe David's zeal for the glory of the living God, his sterling faith in the Almighty, and his wisdom beyond human years, who would not stand amazed at the heights to which the Holy Spirit carried him? And, as we read and ponder the Psalms, which of us does not yearn to draw near to David's inward levels of spiritual exercise?

The same Holy Spirit who was operative at the creation is operative in the work of new creation before Christ came. Exploits of the saints before our Lord's coming can be explained in no other way than this, 'The Spirit of the LORD rushed upon' them. Let us not make a folk-hero or a super-human figure of David. He is another of the saints of Hebrews 11. The Spirit of the Lord was with them all.

As David left Saul's tent, the youth, soon to be the new hero of Israel, had his eye confidently fixed upon his God. The once-popular leader of God's people had lost God's Spirit, God's favour, God's prophet, and God's word for his guidance. With these losses came the loss of courage, joy, peace, and a sound mind. It is a stunning contrast.

Rather, let us crave in our lives the presence of the Holy Spirit, producing the same qualities to be found in David. Let us ask the Father for the Holy Spirit daily. Let us beware of quenching, grieving, and sinning against the Holy Spirit. Saul stands as a monument of warning.

Jesus once said with eloquent brevity, 'Remember Lot's wife.' It would be well to say, 'Remember Saul.' The Spirit of the Lord departed from him. That too is a reality.

Others since his day have shared his experience. Sensitively welcome the Spirit as the holy Guest he is. Fall in step with the Spirit.

5

THE BATTLE IS THE LORD'S

1 Samuel 17:40–18:16

David's comments to his brothers and their fellow-soldiers of Israel and then to Saul in 1 Samuel 17 were not rehearsed speeches. There was no composition of what ought to be said, no contemplation of what others would think of him. His words were an authentic expression of a genuine consciousness of the Almighty. They flowed from impressions of the unique grandeur of God which he had observed in creation. Their depth was taken from David's awareness of the nearness of his God in providence.

As David approached Goliath, making it plain that he had accepted the giant's challenge (*1 Sam.* 17:40), the young man's faith continued to perceive the reality and immanence of the Most High. He strode forward with unfaltering step, his mind poised with the assurance that he was on the Lord's side, and the Lord was by his side.

The giant moved toward David, agitated that a mere boy was sent to fight him. He had looked for a seasoned and decorated warrior in full garb of combat. Instead, a shepherd came to him with sticks, as if to chase away a dog. No words were too contemptuous for Goliath's use; he cursed David by his gods and threatened his swift demise.

1. In the Battle, God Gave David Fearlessness

At the lion-like roar of his foe, the son of Jesse was unshaken. He returned threat for threat. From David there was a difference. With no insult to his enemy's prowess, the youth cried, 'This day the LORD will deliver you into my hand ... And I will give the dead bodies of the host of the Philistines this day to the birds of the air and to the wild beasts ... that all the earth may know that there is a God in Israel, and that all ... may know that the battle is the LORD's' (*1 Sam.* 17:46-47).

This said, the new champion of Israel went about the business-like slaying of a giant! A stone was hurled into the small, unprotected forehead; the foe's sword was seized for cutting off his head – so that everyone may know that the monster of Gath would never again harm anyone.

Many years later Jeremiah would warn, 'Let not ... the mighty man boast in his might' (as did Goliath), 'but let him who boasts boast in this, that he understands and knows me, that I am the LORD' (as did David; see *Jer.* 9:23-24). However, such boasting must not be in the form of words only, but also from heart-acquaintance.

Courage from the Lord cannot be sustained by bravado. It arises only with faith which is exercised in communion with the Maker of heaven and earth. A steady hand in the fight is the result of a steady gaze of faith.

2. In the Battle, God Gave David Trophies

Battlefields are not immaculate and antiseptic. David decapitated Goliath by Goliath's huge sword. As he held the bloody severed head aloft in triumph, the army of Philistia arose as one man in panicked retreat. The same gruesome prize of battle roused the army of Israel to chase the foe. Abner, the captain of the host under Saul, ushered David into the king's presence. As he returned to his king, the lad carried his souvenirs of combat, Goliath's head, armour, and sword.

For some reason David deposited the head at Jerusalem. The Philistine's equipment of war he took to his home. With these trophies he savoured his victory, but his triumph was in and from the Lord.

We live in a day in which multitudes believe that God's only interest in violent warfare is to express disapproval of it. Many suggest that the God of the Old Testament is discredited and that he has been replaced by the New Testament God of only love and peace. Such a view ignores the positive teaching of Romans 13:1–7. There we are told that rulers, bearing the sword in just causes and in defence of the good, are God's agents of justice.

Many pacifists refuse to recognize the depths of evil in the hearts of those rogues who rule aggressive and oppressive states. Others, with the same devotion to non-aggression, are relativists who are angered to hear anyone label one cause 'evil' and another 'good'. The hand of divine providence is not withheld from any war. At times the design of neither combatant is accomplished, but a third design (in the secret will of God) is established. All warriors may be left with 'unintended consequences', to their way of thinking.

Warriors and those they protect should rejoice when the Lord grants victory in their just cause. It is consistent with humble dependence on God to celebrate battlefield triumphs.

David's momentary encounter with Goliath in the theatre of war became the beginning of a new period in his life. For this chapter in his history, God gave David three further gifts, which arrived in connection with the battle and continued until he rose to the throne in Israel.

3. In the Battle, God Gave David Friendship

One who was watching David's conquest that day was Jonathan. Only a short while before (*1 Sam.* 14), at Michmash, Jonathan had single-handedly routed the Philistine army. In that conflict he had fought with faith in the God of Israel, with zeal for the divine Name, yes, and with extraordinary courage, and prevailed. At once, Jonathan recognized in the Bethlehemite the traits which he shared and so admired. That day the Lord knit the hearts of David and Jonathan together in a lifelong, godly, and manly love.

Jonathan took the initiative to forge this friendship. He rejoiced in David's victory, though it captured the limelight which he had once held. David won the attention and affection of the people, which relegated

Jonathan to second place. Nevertheless, the displaced one took steps to make the man of higher reputation his friend. Romans 12:10 advises, 'Love one another with brotherly affection. Outdo one another in showing honour.' If you would have friends, you must show yourself friendly (*Prov.* 18:24).

The crown prince of Israel made a covenant with the shepherd. He gave his clothing and weapons to David as symbols of his devoted comradeship. One day Jonathan would even express agreement with God's will that David should have the crown intended for him! It was a selfless, sacrificial, loyal love for David that would endure until death. Mutual fidelity was pledged that very day, and it proved to be a most satisfying fellowship to both men for a lifetime.

David's life experiences were about to be most trying for a lengthy period of time. As the trials began, God gave him the precious gift of a friend. A faithful friend is a strong defence in adversity, a soothing medicine when one is deeply wounded. Men need friends well chosen from the number who love the Lord. It is clear that Jesus wants to see our love for him worked out in love for the brethren.

4. In the Battle, God Gave David Favour with Israel

As the men were returning home from the battle with the Philistines, women came out from all the towns of Israel, singing, playing instruments, and dancing. 'Saul has struck down his thousands, and David his ten thousands' (*1 Sam.* 18:7). This was their refrain.

David's heroics had captured the imagination and admiration of all Israel. His fame was instantaneously legendary. He was a celebrity! David declared, 'The battle is the LORD's.' He meant it. But the populace longed for a mortal man to trust. They were intoxicated with David and his exploits. He was the theme of their celebration.

King Saul could not ignore a figure so magnificently instrumental in the spectacular deliverance of his nation. He made David instantaneously an officer of high rank in his army. In every campaign to which he was assigned by Saul, David was wise and successful, because the Lord was with him. All his military missions pleased the populace so that his fame increased. He also pleased the officer corps. Ordinarily, these competitive officers had their jealousies. But God gave David favour with them all.

5. In the Battle, God Gave David the Malevolence of the King

Holding the hearts of the crown prince, the women, and the army, David was being prepared to succeed Saul. The ruler of Israel knew that the Lord was with David and that the same Lord had left him. He was afraid of David for good reasons. His fear was agitated by the evil spirit from the Lord.

God's words and acts cannot be denied and opposed without dire consequences to those who hate what the Lord has established. Unbelievers rage against the Bible and against the order God has created on the earth. Those who know the truth of God but suppress that knowledge

(*Rom*. 1:18–20) will only injure themselves, as they hurl themselves against the rock-firm realities which God has decreed and instituted.

Saul knew that God was angry with the aging king and that God's favour was toward the young hero of Israel. However, his conscience could not endure admitting this. He turned all the power of his government against these truths of God, only to break his own bones, as he threw himself against God's truth. Time and again he was forced to admit what his conscience could not endure. This alternate admission and denial is the essence of mad instability.

When Saul heard the women sing of David's prowess being greater than his own, he remarked, 'what more can he have but the kingdom?' (*1 Sam*. 18:8). The greater the applause for David, the more Saul looked askance at him.

At the same instant that God raised David to eminence, the Almighty assigned a gnawing worm to eat at his inner life. He humbly and faithfully served king and nation. God's choice for the throne would not rise to that position of power as quickly as Israel's choice had done. Saul had risen like a rocket, but had now fallen like a stick.

In such a way, many years later, the Son of God would learn obedience through the things which he suffered, before reigning at God's right hand. For David, sharp adversity would heighten trust in God, self-control, and prayerfulness. No sooner would he taste the sweetness of victory over the man from Gath than bitter herbs would reach his lips. The promise of the hand of the king's daughter would be withdrawn. There would come false accusation, separation from home and family, as he was driven into the wilderness, and there was also the treachery of threatened assassination.

Humiliation was David's path to the throne. What would the world's highest prominence and power do to a youth? Had he not discovered the remaining sin deep within the recesses of his heart before being crowned, would he too have made shipwreck of the faith? Does not humiliation sanctify us all? None of us welcomes humiliation. If it is God's instrument to preserve us and to mortify sin, we will one day thank him for even this gift. There will be, however, no excuse for Saul in having brought about the humiliation. The king clearly had no kind motive in his assaults on David.

Just before running toward Goliath, David announced that the battle was the Lord's. We see that demonstrated in the instantaneous death of a mighty warrior at the hands of an untrained youth. We see it in the rout of the Philistine army in a single day. We see it in the sudden burst of exultation throughout Israel. It is so obvious that the Lord gave an unlikely victory in this battle.

For David, a much longer conflict began at once. This second was to be a series of confrontations attended by murky intrigue. For years it appeared that the battle was going against him. This time his enemy would not fall by David's courageous acts. The enemy would not even fall by David's hand. At its conclusion in David's favour, there would be tears, not celebration. Nevertheless, this battle too was the Lord's.

Some battles are sustained until those who fight them are weary unto death. Battles may bring to the victor many a wound with life-long consequences. Divine Providence supervised each phase of David's new conflict and ordained every injustice suffered. Warriors who do not feel any thrill in victory must humbly acknowledge, 'Whate'er my God ordains is right.'

Still, the battle is the Lord's.

6

LOVE AND MARRIAGE

1 Samuel 18:17–19:17

All of life does not have one dimension. This is true even for a young military officer, who is leading troops into combat against the constant raids from a persistently hostile neighbouring state. David would return to Gibeah to report on recent skirmishes. There would be found the infant trappings of a king's court; there would be a few hours taken with his friend Jonathan; there would be young women and the latest social news about young love. For David it was the springtime of manhood.

In a conversation between the king and the young warrior, Saul called David's attention to his elder daughter Merab. A princess! Her father promised to give her hand in marriage to David. A time for the wedding was actually set in making the proposition to David.

Discussion of this marriage makes no mention of love. David seemed to be genuinely troubled by social considerations. He was a poor man, starting out in life, unable to offer a dowry for a princess. His father was a farmer in Bethlehem. Who was he to become son-in-law to the king? Recognizing that David's hesitations arose from a sense of inferior social standing, Saul buttressed his hopes.

However, God, who searches all hearts, discloses to us the motives of Saul, which were fed by the dark spirit sent to the king to torment him. The monarch said that he only wanted David's loyalty to himself and to Jehovah in return for his daughter's hand and heart. Like the serpent of old, he lied. His desire was that David should die. He knew the Philistines would hear that David had become son-in-law to the king of Israel. Their hatred of the Jews would mark out David as their most wanted man. Saul even took God's name in vain with this ploy.

The cat was playing with the mouse. This cat would use affairs of the heart to betray his own daughter and the loyal soldier. Those who think that the social tragedies connected with young love will be solved by having parents who will make all arrangements for marriage, have not considered the depravity of parents. Their self-interest has often led to their children's lifelong misery. Saul would have been willing to make Merab a young widow to satisfy his envious malice.

At the very time when David had been promised union with Merab, her father gave her to another man, who is now utterly unknown apart from this marriage. What talk of these events would have run through the court in Gibeah! What embarrassment to the young captain! The cat's claw is very sharp.

Still the social contacts continued. New rumours began. These were more interesting. The word 'love' was being mentioned. As yet, the king had no awareness, but the gossip was that Michal, Saul's younger daughter, loved David. Romance is important to marriage. Husbands are expected to love their wives. Young women should have their affections engaged with the ones they marry.

This is one of the great mysteries propounded in Scripture by the words of Agur. 'The way of a man with a virgin' is too wonderful for him to understand (*Prov.* 30:18-19). Even after having the experience, the chemistry of love cannot be explained. This is why love stories ever grip us. They are wondrous. When the eyes of the young meet, as words are exchanged (in teasing or serious discourse), when notes are passed and read breathlessly to catch some hint of shared fondness, when meetings are arranged through intermediaries, a mutual attraction grows and a deep interest of affection is ignited. How did David and Michal meet? Was Jonathan a willing fan to these glowing embers?

This time a romance was underway before the king stirred the kettle. It was the princess who sent word to the king that she was in love. So it should be. If parents have their advice sought or their consent requested, the will of the children must be a primary concern. When Abraham's servant asked for the hand of Rebekah in marriage for Isaac, it came down to this question, asked of the young lady, 'Will you go with this man?' (*Gen.* 24:58).

This romance pleased Saul. It pleased him because he had been able to bring pain to David once: now he may destroy him. The selfish tyrant cared nothing about the destruction of his daughter's heart and life in the process.

Saul again purposed to give a daughter to David as the means of inciting Philistines to kill him. He gave David a second opportunity to be his son-in-law. This time, as a dowry he asked proof of David's having personally slain one hundred Philistines. He salivated at the anticipation that one heathen man of war would have the better of the son of Jesse. With what a dark countenance must he have greeted the news that David had quickly killed twice the number of foes requested!

It is an irony of history and of the Scripture record that Saul's is not the only heart so black with evil motive and deceit. David in this scene was done an enormous injustice. When David sat upon the throne, many years later, he used precisely the same devices to slay Uriah as were employed by Saul against himself. David could be Saul toward a soldier loyal to his king. Where, through the good providence of God, Saul failed, David succeeded in the deed of murder. Little do we realize that the same seeds of wickedness, which, in the hearts of other men, bring stabbing pain to us, lie within our own fallen nature. What a great business it is to 'Keep your heart with all vigilance'! (*Prov.* 4:23).

David secured a home in Gibeah. There was a wedding day. The national hero married the princess. The ceremony is not described. Was it similar to Psalm 45, written by David? There, a wedding procession began at the groom's home. Riding upon a horse, in full military splendour, attended by noble men and women, we may imagine, he processed through the streets of Gibeah to Michal's house. There she nervously awaited her mighty lover. She was all beautiful within and without. The bride was taken by her husband, and they rode through the streets to shouts of joy and acclamation, back to David's home. There a feast had been prepared for family and friends. The banns of marriage had been publicly proclaimed in the streets and toasted at the feast.

Notwithstanding, they did not live happily ever after! Michal's father was interfering and manipulating. With words he gave his daughter to David. In fact, he would not acknowledge David's headship over her. The king expected his daughter's first loyalty. Oh! The evils done in young marriages by the improper interventions of parents!

It is clear from Scripture that God advises newly-weds to rejoice in their new-found intimacy (*Prov.* 5:18–19). The first year is so foundational to a lifelong marriage that the Lord advises that even national emergencies should not interrupt the mutual happiness of newly-weds (*Deut.* 24:5).

Saul, however, intended to dash the hopes of his daughter's love. He schemed for her to lay her beloved in the grave and never see her wedding day. When the marriage was consummated, the father-in-law moved from secret designs to spoken ones. Saul attempted to enlist his son and all his trusted servants to aid in David's murder. Now warnings began to come to the ears of David from Jonathan, and no doubt to Michal from family members or friends at court.

Jonathan wisely and boldly rebuked his father for his murderous intent within the family. Saul seemed to give heed to his son and swore on oath to Jehovah that David would not die by his hand. Thus, Jonathan patched up a very serious family feud. Following upon Jonathan's mediation, David continued to play his harp to soothe Saul's fevered moods. All too soon, however, the warrior-king had thrust his spear at his son-in-law. David was forced to flee from the ruler's presence to the relative safety of his newly-established home.

Immediately, royal guards were dispatched to David and Michal's home to keep them under surveillance until morning, when David should be killed. Inside, the young man and wife received friendly advice. It became clear to Michal that David must flee for his life in the next few hours or die. Truly loving her new husband, she chose him over her father. She created a furtive plan of escape and an appearance of David's being sick in bed, while David ran for his life.

In the morning a bloodthirsty king insisted that the 'sick' David be carried on his bed into his presence, so that the monarch might have the pleasure of personally killing him.

When Michal's ruse was uncovered, the poor young wife was left alone to face her mad father's ravings. Under the pressure of the event, Michal diverted the wrath of Saul from herself by inventing the lie that her young husband had threatened her life.

Few young husbands and wives have had such stormy first months of marriage. When the home atmosphere cooled again, David and Michal must have had discussions of what transpired and what was said while they were so cruelly separated. Is it possible that these conversations strained their relationship in ways that never healed?

Saul kept David on the run from home and from wife for years. During that time, David entered that Satanic trap to which other Old Testament saints were blind: polygamy. Multiple marriages kept so many homes in turmoil and grief. Jealousies between wives, half-brothers and half-sisters, in the family would plague David to the very end.

Michal would have known that her husband, the hero of Israel, was the theme of every maiden's song. How the girls would watch his actions! How their romantic dreams would have been daggers to her! Some would even become rivals within her household. All of this distortion of home life was, in some measure, her father's marriage gift. He did not even grant to her the early months of joy which marriage should bring.

Nor did David ever experience the normal, or divinely ordered, institution of marriage. Was the Bathsheba saga in some way an outworking of Saul's sin? David had his responsibilities for it and faced them. Yet the twistings of sin are intricate. Although we must not shift blame for our transgressions, there may be many who work at weaving the webs which entrap us.

As we review the miseries of sin which stalk us, there is much evil and weakness to be found in our own hearts. How we must cry to God to cleanse us through the mercy and merits of our Lord Jesus Christ!

We also, as did David, pass through dark labyrinths of temptation which are built by others to ensnare us. Daily prayer to be delivered from evil is more necessary than we know. How vital are these prayers for marriage and family!

How we wish home and hearth could be a refuge from fierce spiritual battles! Yet, often the greatest battles are fought in that very society. May God grant to his people an ever-increasing growth in the graces needed to live with our families as he would have us live.

7

A SANCTUARY FROM OPPRESSION

1 Samuel 19:18–24

David's home in Gibeah, to which he had brought his wife, Michal, was surrounded by spies sent from her father, King Saul. Their chief mission was not to gather information on the newly-weds, but rather to contain David overnight. In the morning, as we have seen, Saul intended to kill the commander of his own army, who was utterly loyal to him, and who was the most skilful field-officer in his employ. Under cover of darkness David's young princess bride planned and assisted his escape through a window.

As an experienced warrior, David's immediate attention had to focus on eluding the king's troopers. Yet, in doing so, his mind must have also been set on the direction of his flight. Agitating within David's spirit was the question he would soon ask of Jonathan: 'What have I done? What is my guilt? And what is my sin before your father, that he seeks my life?' (*1 Sam.* 20:1). He was being tormented by intense and ruthless injustice. If it had come from the heathen, it would have been expected. Rather, it came from those by whose side he had bravely served in the high cause of God's glory and kingdom. In addition, at that moment, the Lord's anointed had also to distance himself from his dearest earthly friend, Jonathan. Where else could he find respite from a hailstorm of abuse?

Only two miles from Gibeah was Ramah, the hometown of the great and aged prophet of Israel, who had anointed David. There would be an oasis of safety, counsel, and consolation! Through the night David made his lonely trek to Samuel. Late into the hours of the night, David told the man of God 'all that Saul had done to him' (*1 Sam.* 19:18).

Sometimes ministers of the Word, even in the highest ecclesiastical positions, are nonetheless powerless to put an end to injustice. However, a sympathetic hearing, words of advice, and an assurance of God's assistance are like cool water poured on the burning sands of persecution. Expressed compassion for Christ's weak and harassed sheep is a vital part of the ministry. Although this was only a momentary interlude for David as a fugitive, this consultation with Samuel would make a lasting impression upon him.

Some who hold office in the church think that they are too busy with more important matters to be turned aside to issues of injustice and oppression. No spiritual leader in Israel was more prominent than Samuel, or more burdened with responsibilities than he. His schedule was crowded with the most crucial opportunities for preaching and teaching. He then held the top post in the administration of the kingdom of God on earth. However, when a harassed sheep of his flock arrived at his door, other matters were laid aside. Night and day he stood by David in his crisis. Supporting the weak was a high priority of the moment. Samuel did what he could to defend David against slander, lies, and threats of injury. These tools for abuse of power were now fully employed against this youngest son of Jesse.

As a shepherd, David had learned the great importance of carrying the lambs in his bosom (cf. *Isa.* 40:11). He had discovered that the ewes with young must not be harshly driven, but gently led. Protective tenderness, shown by individual attention, was required for the wellbeing of any flock. No blind eye must be turned to the injured or assaulted (*Ezek.* 34). The wounded must be bound up, and the helpless, in the clutches of the bear, must be delivered, even at risk to the shepherd.

In the past David had played the shepherd. Now, during that long night and the following day, David was the object of Samuel's ministrations. He was the sheep, the prophet the shepherd. What is true in the flock is true in the kingdom.

It is good to suffer injustice in order to understand the importance of delivering others from oppression. Could it be that, many years later, David did not so much think of his own example as a shepherd-king over Israel, but rather of his being a sheep in distress, helped by the shepherd, Samuel, when he wrote the memorable words, 'He who rules over men must be just' (*2 Sam.* 23:3, NKJV)? It is the first qualification he mentions for anyone who would rule in home, business, church, or community, equity and fairness administered in the fear of God!

These qualities would mark the reign of the Messiah, the Chief Shepherd (*Psa.* 72). He would vanquish all abusers of authority. For example, Jesus heard a report that rulers of the synagogue had crudely and unjustly banished from their assembly a recent beneficiary of our Lord's mercy. Jesus dropped other matters at hand and rushed to console and strengthen the weak disciple, so insignificant in the eyes of earthly leaders (*John* 9).

In the morning Samuel and David went to Naioth, an unusual rural community on the fringe of Ramah. Here Samuel had gathered a society of prophets. This is the first appearance in Scripture of a 'school of prophets'. Such communes continued to exist into the days of Elijah and Elisha.

It appears that Samuel gathered, discipled, and directed young, godly men for the purpose of widespread ministry in Israel. Thus, from the flame of Samuel's spirituality, many lesser fires were lit. The priesthood had been greatly weakened at the destruction of Shiloh. Later, it would be more severely damaged by a violent attack from Saul. A new institution was being raised up to train men to teach the nation and to lead them in the worship of their God. Into this unique fellowship Samuel led the great psalm-singer of Israel.

Saul was relentless! His effective intelligence units soon reported that David was at Naioth (*1 Sam.* 19:19). Saul sent his storm troopers to Naioth to seize him. However, they became helpless in the presence of Samuel and the group of prophets at worship. A similar failure of mission befell a second and a third contingent of Saul's crack troops. Finally, Saul himself was neutralized at Naioth (*1 Sam*. 19:20–24).

There was no conflict in Naioth. David was simply in the midst of a band of worshipping prophets, with Samuel leading the praises of God. As Saul intruded on this scene of devotion amidst the noise of horses' hooves and clanking armour, he and his forces came under the powerful influences of the Holy Spirit; thereby the monarch was made incapable of executing his murderous designs against the Lord's anointed. In this Spirit-filled assembly he and his men were compelled to act as did the prophets. Not only did the prophets engage in the extraordinary gift of prophesying, so also did the men of war and the king, who was pursuing his own evil purposes.

It would be well for us to pause and meditate on the fact that engaging in the exercise of extraordinary spiritual gifts is no sign that one possesses spiritual and saving grace. Often in Scripture ungodly men are used by the Holy Spirit to prophesy genuinely. It was so with Balaam. In Numbers 22–24, Balaam prophesied truth from the Lord, although he was forever afterward a prominent example of the man who has forsaken the right way (*2 Pet*. 2:15). Heathen soldiers were instruments of prophecy to Gideon (*Judg*. 7:13–14). There is every reason to believe that Judas cast out demons along with the other apostles (*Luke* 9:1). Jesus' words are very sobering on this subject: 'And then will I declare to them, "I never knew you; depart from me, you workers of lawlessness"' (*Matt.* 7:23). Let none who claim to prophesy take any comfort from that fact. It is no evidence of a heart that is right with God.

Where there is Spirit-filled worship, wickedness may be restrained, even when the wicked are left in their sins. A fear of God, which may not save those who have evil purposes in their hearts, may yet compel such unbelievers to fall on their faces and declare that God is really among the saints (*1 Cor.* 14:25). Even demons, in the presence of Christ, trembled as they owned his lordship!

Never did God so dramatically prepare for David a table of rich spiritual delights in the very presence of his enemies (*Psa.* 23:5) as at Naioth. There the Lord made even his ferocious enemies to be at peace with him (*Prov.* 16:7). The mouths of lions were stopped in the place of worship.

Saul's experience may frighten those who contemplate it. For months an evil spirit had controlled the king's behaviour. Suddenly, the Holy Spirit rushed upon him, bringing an even more powerful influence over him for a few hours.

Thus he 'tasted the heavenly gift' and 'shared in the Holy Spirit' (*Heb.* 6:4). He was under divine compulsions which outwardly produced the appearance of his being just like the most godly of men. This caused the astonished exclamation, 'Is Saul also among the prophets?' (*1 Sam.* 19:24). Yet, when the immediate experience ended, he remained under the powers of the evil spirit, captive to its will. He was all the more distant from God and from true religion.

Similar patterns have surprised observers of powerful spiritual awakenings. When the Spirit moves in an extraordinary way to create new hearts in many elect sinners, others, who are present at the worship in which this occurs, are temporarily moved by God's Spirit to fall in with the external signs of the Spirit's operations. But alas! When the meetings are ended, a number, who were obviously touched by the Spirit's working, are not permanently transformed.

Some have been hastily dogmatic in saying that these cases of observable religious impressions are Satanic counterfeits or mere human imitations. Saul was not under the influence of the evil spirit at that moment, nor did he fabricate his behaviour to follow the prophets. 'The Spirit of God came upon him also' (*1 Sam*. 19:23). Hebrews 6:4–6 teaches this third possibility of interpretation. In fact, the most hopeless hypocrites are those who have felt the operations of the Spirit of God, but not in a saving manner. From this body of men and women, who have been touched by powerful heavenly forces, but who remain unconverted, have come 'many antichrists' (*1 John* 2:18-20), the most virulent haters of Christianity.

For David, that night and day in Naioth demonstrated that all was not dark in Israel. He had lived with the worst of Israel at Gibeah. No confidence could be placed in Israel's princes. He was now conversant with the best streams of spirituality in the nation. Did he first meet Nathan there when both were young men? To be sure, he was strengthened in the inner man by the wave of the future found in the holy brotherhood.

So should pilgrims ever find within their churches. There should be an atmosphere distinct from the world in which the saints live. There should be spiritual worship and fellowship. The true church, under the Spirit's filling, is the wave of the future for our sin-tired world.

Let us pray that God would give us churches where old and young commune together in the near presence of the Lord, as did Samuel and David.

Ask God that we may again see ministries under which the wildest of ungodly men are introduced to the more lofty experiences for which our humanity was made. Saul temporarily had his resistance to God broken in a glimpse of high spiritual reality. God grant that we may see the most determined rebels against God helplessly humbled before their Maker by the compulsions of the Holy Spirit. It is better that men be stripped bare now than that they be made naked before him with whom we have to do, and this for the first time, in the day of judgment.

8

FAREWELL TO GIBEAH, HOME, AND FRIENDS!

1 Samuel 20

From Naioth, David returned to Gibeah. The son of Jesse was then fully convinced that Saul had a fixed determination to murder him. Observing the king among the prophets, caught up momentarily in the ecstasies of spiritual worship, did not sway David from his correct judgment of the old ruler. Retracing his steps to Gibeah was, then, a most dangerous course for him.

Saul, even in his madness, had a lucid grasp of many realities. As God and his prophet Samuel retreated from the king, David was ascending in power and popularity before Israel (*1 Sam.* 18:8). This young man was increasingly the greatest threat to Saul's ambition for a family dynasty (*1 Sam.* 20:31). The Benjamite ruler had an incisive comprehension of the affairs of state. Years before, he had been reluctantly drafted to be the first king of Israel. With some youthful reticence and humility he ascended the throne. He was to be a servant to God and to God's people, aided by the Holy Spirit.

A pinnacle of leadership (such as that of servant-shepherd) is also in some sense a pinnacle of power. Planning and executing designs for a kingdom give one a feeling of mastery. Though his ability to achieve his ends may be due to the potency of the Almighty himself attending his servant, it may still seem a very satisfying experience to be in the place of extensive influence. Those who have lost former prestige and authority may feel bereft (as did Job in chapter 29 of his book). By degrees the inclination to servanthood declines in some, as a quest for control increases, just at the time when the control is slipping away.

Saul was, at this stage of life, consumed with resolve to shape the future of the kingdom. Who had laboured so much as he to establish the nation? Who had invested and risked so much to form this rising society of the Jews? The work *he* had begun would *not* fall into the hands of a Bethlehem farm boy!

As David made his way back to Gibeah, he still could not explain what was happening to him. When a trusted ally and brother becomes one's enemy, there is an inward wrenching which prevents one from being able to account for such a radical change. To Saul's dying day, David never verbalized the obvious source of the king's enmity.

David returned to what, for him, was the most dangerous spot on earth. It would be only a visit of four days, and those would be spent in hiding. However, he felt compelled to consult with his dear friend, Jonathan.

Perhaps Jonathan could provide the much-needed explanation of his father's designs. Had David done something to offend Saul? Could he possibly make amends (*1 Sam.* 20:1)?

The discussion with Jonathan did not begin well in David's view. He asked his closest friend on earth why the king was seeking to take away his life. Saul's son denied that David was under attack (*1 Sam.* 20:2)! This could only have compounded David's misery. His friend did not believe him, but instead trusted the explanations of David's enemy! Did Jonathan think that his friend was hallucinating? Did he think him paranoid?

Some men are so charitable in their judgments of others that they cannot detect the most evil behaviour in people until that evil is directed against them. A short time later, when Saul hurled a spear at Jonathan, then the realization dawned that Saul really was David's determined foe (*1 Sam.* 20:33).

How was David going to bring his friend to see the truth? He began with an oath: 'But truly, as the LORD lives and as your soul lives, there is but a step between me and death' (*1 Sam.* 20:3). Such a solemn comment convinced Jonathan of David's deep seriousness, although it did not win him to David's opinion. Not yet prepared to see David's danger, nor to believe in his father's injustice, the loyal friend promised to do whatever David asked, in order to investigate this charge (*1 Sam.* 20:4).

David devised a scheme which God blessed to open the blinded eyes of Jonathan. Though God acted swiftly in this situation, some live a long time with friends who think them to be emotionally imbalanced, because they describe their experiences of oppression.

In all ages God's people have joined family feasts and community celebrations to religious ceremonies. David returned to Gibeah at the time of New Moon sacrifices (*Num.* 10:10; 28:11–15), at which Saul would expect his family and chief officers to attend the feast at court. David asked Jonathan to tell his father that David could not attend, because the house of Jesse had a similar celebration, and David's older brother had ordered him to be in Bethlehem (*1 Sam.* 20:5–8). Secret signals were agreed upon in the event that Jonathan could not find a safe way to meet with David after securing the desired information (*1 Sam.* 20:11–23).

Some brood about the fact that righteous men speak falsehoods at certain times in scriptural accounts. Here, David would not be in Bethlehem, but asked Jonathan to say that he was. When pursued by an unrelenting murderer, or in the midst of war, or while conducting espionage against a mortal enemy, fastidious honesty is not required. Evasion and tactics of battle demand deceit. Fools must be answered according to their folly.

Jonathan and David chose a safe hiding place for David, and agreed on a code which would inform David of Jonathan's findings. While they were laying plans, Jonathan made some most remarkable comments to David. His heartfelt words flowed with astounding insights, or with premonition, or even with prophetic guidance. Jonathan delivered two oaths (one self-maledictory) promising to report to David and to send him away safely (*1 Sam.*

20:12–13). He included a benediction, 'May the LORD be with you, as he has been with my father' (*1 Sam.* 20:13). Did he then realize that David was to be king?

In this same conversation Jonathan formed a mutual vow between David's household and his own. For this purpose Jonathan anticipated a day when all David's enemies would be cut off. He extracted from David a vow to show kindness to Jonathan's house forever.

What gave such insights to Jonathan? David feared for his life. Jonathan was certain that God would watch over and protect David. At that moment Jonathan was a prince, to whom his father intended to give the kingdom. At the same time everyone else realized that David was marked for death. Yet Jonathan was eager to make a pact in which David would bless the prince's household in the future! This is nearly as amazing as the thief on the cross, who acknowledged Jesus' ability to bless him at the very instant of our Lord's deepest humiliation. Jonathan contentedly contemplated a reverse of fortunes for David and for himself.

It is not a mere wish that is expressed in Jonathan's 'Go in peace', but a confidence that the Lord would go with his anointed one. Christians today should make greater use of sincere benedictions. The book of Ruth gives abundant examples of this ancient habit among the saints. So too do the New Testament epistles. Love and goodwill may be verbalized between friends by prayerful benedictions.

Benedictions also bring great encouragement to those who receive them, no matter what their condition at the moment. A few words of benediction can make deep impressions.

When Jonathan carried through David's stratagem, Saul immediately recognized it as a ruse (*1 Sam.* 20:30). He insisted that Jonathan personally bring David to him, suspecting (correctly) that the rival to his throne was hiding nearby. 'He shall surely die', said Saul. Voices were rising in the presence of guests as a royal family argument erupted. Jonathan pleaded for David's innocence as he had done before. The king cursed his own son and even his own wife. Finally, the king hurled a spear at the heir apparent, who stalked out of the 'celebration' in 'fierce anger'. In a burst of insanity, Saul sought to kill his only heir at the very moment he insisted on securing the throne of Israel for his family. Shouting, cursing, attempted murder, resolve to murder, all within the family, were the sauces of the royal family feast that day. What a tragic day it was for Israel!

Saul's behaviour on this occasion is a leading negative biblical example, serving as a commentary on Ephesians 6:4, 'Fathers, do not provoke your children to anger.' As fire kindles fire, so anger kindles anger. Saul's fierce anger toward Jonathan sparked fierce anger within Jonathan. So it ever is in managing children. Fathers, more than mothers, are tempted to treat their children with unreasonable severity and harshness. Fathers who cannot control their own tempers in disciplining their children will fail to control the spirits of their sons and daughters. Saul's tongue-lashing of Jonathan with cursing and name-calling only aroused anger, not submission to his will.

Abusive assaults on children have the opposite fruit from that which parents desire. Humiliation of Jonathan in the presence of others challenged his manhood to react against his father. In Saul's extreme example lies a world of heart-searching for parents.

Jonathan, however, was ever the selfless friend! Scripture tells us that, even at the moment of receiving enormous personal embarrassment and unjust assault, his motive for anger was that 'he was grieved for David, because his father had disgraced him' (*1 Sam.* 20:34). Oh, for such grace to be lovingly attentive to the mistreatment of others, more than to our own wounds! Lord, teach us how to be Christian friends!

On the next morning Jonathan gave the secret signals to David, as he had promised. As his mission was completed, it was apparent to both Jonathan and David that enemies had not followed Jonathan. There were a few moments in which the friends said 'Goodbye'. It is a most moving scene to watch as these two military heroes and soul-mates express their farewells.

David began. He 'fell on his face to the ground and bowed three times' (*1 Sam.* 20:41). He was recognizing that Jonathan was a princely man. Loyal in carrying out his promises, Jonathan had placed himself in grave danger for his friend. Now David had the great satisfaction of knowing that the man, whom he loved the most on earth, *understood* his plight.

It was not that he looked to Jonathan to deliver him. David's visit to Gibeah was worth the hazard to secure his friend's full comprehension of his position. No other man would ever have more of David's esteem. He expressed it emotionally.

The two men kissed and they wept together at the tragedy that had befallen them both. David wept the more at the thought of their parting. Jonathan voiced another profound benediction. Then David 'rose and departed, and Jonathan went into the city' (*1 Sam.* 20:42). Only once more would the two meet in life, and then only briefly. David was now a permanent fugitive so long as Saul was king. Jonathan turned back to the tensions of Gibeah. David went alone into the wilderness.

9

IN THE WILDERNESS–1: OUTCASTS

1 Samuel 21 & 22

David had begun to walk a very lonely path. It was a journey of boundless danger. He was loyal to Saul, the Lord's anointed. He was devoted to the people of Saul, seeking their safety and prosperity. He was dedicated to the institutions Saul led, the prophetic school, the priestly tabernacle, the national government of Israel. Yet David was the object of Saul's fierce oppression. The king was doing his utmost to employ the people and institutions of his nation to destroy David.

If David were to strike back against the conspiracy amassed against him, he would be assaulting the people and institutions that he most loved. He found in Samuel an ear sympathetic to his dilemma, and another in Jonathan.

However, each time he confided in someone about the mounting plot against him, he succeeded only in bringing his confidant under the same danger and abuse which he was suffering. These chapters in Samuel depict a still very young man attempting to negotiate the meanderings of this labyrinthine trial.

Such is the plight of many in modern times who have received unjust and oppressive treatment from churches and church officers, even though the latter may remain on the side of truth. To remain under deformed government would only bring more wounds upon the distressed person. If complaints are sounded, the foundations of the cause of truth may be shaken. When one flees in relative silence, his every act is misinterpreted.

Such a fate has befallen David even down to our present day. Modern commentators, not appreciating the intricate weavings of this web of testing, accuse him of sin and of being far from God at this time in his life. Yet there was no way for the young warrior safely to stand still or to move on. Nor was there any way to speak up with the truth. Life-threatening hazards and kingdom-menacing risks attended every option of action and inaction, of speaking and of being silent.

Only a few days earlier David had been in Naioth. Yesterday he had been hiding in Ramah. Today the hunted had arrived at Nob, a town midway between Ramah and Jerusalem, within distant view of the latter. There was the high priest, Ahimelech, the great-grandson of Eli, with his ephod. The tabernacle was now without the ark of the covenant. Worship in Israel had been so disrupted!

David's approach alarmed Ahimelech. The circumstances of his coming were most unusual. A great captain was alone and unarmed. Everyone in leadership knew that an evil spirit tormented Saul. The throne was unstable, unreliable, and subject to vast changes with every mood swing of the monarch. Suspicion was in the air. An unsavoury character, Doeg the Edomite, was lurking in the shadows of the tabernacle. With one eye on Doeg, neither Ahimelech nor David could enter into an open or confidential fellowship with the other. David had brought a few trusted companions from Ramah, but they did not appear at the tabernacle. Subterfuge was on every side.

David requested bread from the high priest. He and his men were in need of nourishment. The only bread at the tabernacle was the 'holy bread'. Each Sabbath day twelve flat cakes of bread, hot from the oven, were placed on golden trays on the golden table in the sanctuary. There were two rows of six loaves each, one loaf for each tribe of Israel. Levitical law required that no one eat this bread except consecrated priests. Yet, neither Ahimelech nor David had any conscience against suspending this ceremonial rule to meet human needs.

Later our Lord Jesus Christ would approvingly call attention to this historic account of Ahimelech having mercifully met the needs of David and his men in this way (*Matt.* 12:1–8; *Mark* 2:23–28). The Saviour did so to rebuke the legalistic strictness of the Pharisees with regard to keeping the Sabbath in such a way as to leave no room for a merciful meeting of human necessity during their observances.

David also requested a weapon, and he received Goliath's sword. This symbol of God's having delivered the nation from a great enemy was being kept with the ephod.

Then the refugee asked the high priest to enquire of the Lord on his behalf. This a high priest would do with the Urim and Thummim. All of these requests were made under the guise of his being on a mission for Saul. None of these ministries of Ahimelech to David escaped the careful notice of Doeg.

From Nob, David and his few men left Israel for the imagined safety of Philistia, the land of their enemies. With no refuge among the people of God, they travelled to Gath, to the court of Achish, ruler of that city-state, where they hoped to beg for asylum. Sadly, when the church inflicts abuse on the citizens of God's kingdom, there is no alternative but for the rejected ones to seek greater kindness from a heartless world.

If David thought that his military exploits against the Philistines would have been forgotten in Gath, he was too naïve. If he guessed that the story of Saul's vendetta against him would win him a welcome, as it would do for other lieutenants of a neighbouring ruler, he was dreaming. Members of the court of Achish at once rehearsed David's history and that with bitter memories. As the murmuring grew, so did David's fear. He then acted the part of an insane man. This ploy incited the disgust of Achish, who wanted David out of his sight. Soon David and his friends were on the road back to Judah. When David would later become a warlord with six hundred troops, he would return to Achish to negotiate a refuge from a position of strength and with far better results (*1 Sam.* 27).

This time David and his few soldier-friends discussed wilderness strongholds in Judah where there might be long-term safety for them. They settled into the cave of Adullam. By this time David's parents and brothers were also suffering from the king's suspicions and surveillance. They were a marked family in the community. The family retreated to Adullam where they could protect one another. Some who are marked for ostracism by modern churches also find their families mistreated with them.

Then there began an amazing movement. Up to this time, David was one who was 'wandering about in deserts and mountains, and in dens and caves of the earth' (*Heb.* 11:38). One by one, other men began to attach themselves to him. Injustice is usually not isolated. It becomes a way of life for authorities who begin to practise abusive measures. Everyone who was distressed by the oppressive and self-centred ways of Saul and his Doeg-like inner circle began to gather with David. The bankrupt and the embittered joined him at Adullam. Before long David had a force of four hundred men, then six hundred.

These were the outcasts from the camp of Israel. To Israel's leadership they were a useless people. As Jesus later was to gather sinners, tax collectors, and prostitutes as followers, David became a warlord over hundreds. From this 'rabble' came David's chief officers when he later rose to the throne of the kingdom. With these who joined him outside the camp, David the captain began to do exploits.

David, with his fighting force, began to defend law and order within the reach of their influence. Raids were made out of their stronghold to defeat Philistine forces that made incursions into Judah. By these lightning offensives, Jews were delivered from destruction of their crops and plunder of their towns. Then the mini-army would again disappear within the wilderness.

2 Samuel 23:8–34 and 1 Chronicles 11:10–47 give us a romantic insight into the camp life of these young heroes of Israel. Stories of their legendary feats would be told and retold around their camp fires, stories such as:

1. *Benaiah* once faced a giant of an Egyptian in combat. He was over nine feet tall. The enemy giant held a spear like a weaver's beam. Yet Benaiah, carrying only a staff, took the offensive. He plucked the spear out of the big man's hands and killed the Egyptian with his own weapon.

2. *Eleazar* one day, serving as an advance scout, came upon a Philistine force set in battle array. While still alone, Eleazar hurled himself into the large formation of Philistines. Hacking right and left with his sword until it clave to his hand, he drove the whole Philistine army into panicked retreat.

3. *Jashobeam* in one day killed three hundred Philistines with his spear. Can you imagine the strength expended in such action?

4. One wintry day, with snow on the ground, the army of David found a lion trapped in a pit into which it had fallen. In a flash, *Benaiah* climbed into the pit and killed the lion with a hand weapon.

What an *esprit de corps* grew in this young military brotherhood! However, not all who came were soldiers. Gad, a seer or prophet, joined David. Perhaps they had met at Naioth. Gad would be with David until his old age. This prophet would record a history of David's reign, which would serve as a source-book for our biblical records.

David and his men travelled to Mizpah of Moab. There the son of Jesse placed his parents under the care of the King of Moab. After all, the young warlord had a soft spot in his heart for the nation of his great grandmother, 'Ruth the Moabite', who chose Israel's God to be her own. David would never forget the protective care of the Moabite king in his hour of uncertainties.

After a time, the prophet Gad delivered a message from the Lord that the little army should not stay at Adullam. Thus they began to range through the forest of Hereth.

One day a breathless priest named Abiathar, son of the high priest Ahimelech, rode into the camp. He brought with him a gruesome tale of the new heights to which bloodshed by King Saul had risen. With what grim faces the men listened as Abiathar recounted the events. Saul had been holding court under a tamarisk tree in Gibeah. When he had learned that David and a band of soldiers were roaming the forest, the king had flown into a self-pitying rage. (He seldom ever heard the name of David without twisting the news into a theory of conspiracy.)

'Hear now, people of Benjamin; will the son of Jesse give every one of you fields and vineyards, will he make you all commanders of thousands and commanders of hundreds, that all of you have conspired against me? No one discloses to me when my son makes a covenant with the son of Jesse. None of you is sorry for me or discloses to me that my son has stirred up my servant against me, to lie in wait, as at this day.' (Family and fellow clan members are all suspect; *1 Sam.* 22:7–8.)

Most were shocked into silence by the unfounded suspicion of the king. Doeg realized that this was a moment of opportunity to gain influence and wealth from Saul. He told only what was factual. Yet, understanding the fantasies of his ruler, he intentionally allowed the facts he reported to be woven into the speculative conjectures of his now prejudiced leader. So do some men always climb into favour by the misfortunes of others. And thus are facts made into lies.

Then Doeg revealed that David had been to Nob where Ahimelech had helped David. So Saul summoned all the priests of Nob. The monarch rudely addressed the high priest, who held the second most lofty position in Israel. Ahimelech was accused of conspiracy against Saul. The priest made a calm and reasonable defence. It was to no avail. Unjust rulers do not listen to reason. Saul ordered the guards standing by to kill the priests on the spot.

Fearing God, the guards would not lift a finger against God's priesthood. Trusted Doeg had no such scruples. Unholy obedience followed the holy disobedience! He shed the blood of eighty-five priests that day. Then Doeg laid waste the entire city of Nob; women, infants and cattle were slain. Years earlier, Saul had not been able to bring himself to slay all the Amalekites and their cattle. Now he obliterated both priesthood and town. Not a soul was left but Abiathar who had escaped to give the account.

As David listened to the priest, his soul must have been filled with a mixture of anger and sorrow. That night

David composed Psalm 52. Here were recorded the painful memories of the thoughts he had had on that day in the tabernacle with Ahimelech. One glance at Doeg, and David had known that the sleazy Edomite would tell Saul of the exchanges between the high priest and the runaway son-in-law of the king. For this reason, David had kept his true situation hidden from Ahimelech. He had not involved the priest in his desertion of Ramah.

Now there came a sickening realization to David. Mere association with him was a crime in the eyes of the king. Conversation with the son of Jesse and common human kindnesses to him were a death sentence. David assured Abiathar that he was safe in the tragic bond of fellowship in the wilderness: 'He who seeks my life seeks your life' (*1 Sam.* 22:23). The one remaining priest of Nob could live in the camp without fear. With a bit less violence, modern church leaders have, in the same way, assumed guilt by association in judging any who have dared to speak to those marked as troublesome.

10

IN THE WILDERNESS–2: GOD'S PROVIDENCE

1 Samuel 23 & 24

David and his six hundred warriors were roaming through the rugged and thinly-populated regions south of Jerusalem, between Philistia on the west and the Dead Sea on the east. In these regions were Adullam, Keilah, the Wilderness of Ziph, the Wilderness of Maon, Hebron, Carmel, and Engedi. Much of the area was pockmarked with steep cliffs, deep ravines, and limestone caverns—many places to find concealment from Saul's predatory army. Still, they were operating within one long day's march of the king's capital, Gibeah.

Saul's rule over God's people was coming to an end. The aging king had alienated the prophets by stubborn disobedience to the word of the Lord. He had slaughtered much of the priesthood and destroyed the town where tabernacle worship had been conducted. Isolated from God's servants and the means of grace, evil Saul had the company of evil spirits who manipulated his moods, his words, and his actions. Under demonic influence Saul became a man driven to kill his God-appointed successor.

1. Formative Providence

Working above and through the decisions of the heroes and the villains of history is the God of unsearchable wisdom. Ordering and controlling all events and creatures in this world, the Lord is directing all things great and small to accomplish his holy purposes. Divine sovereign government is firmly guiding the ship of his created world to accomplish his wise, just, and good designs. Each event has meaning.

As the author of all that is good, the Lord was working in David to will and to do of his divine good pleasure (*Phil.* 2:13). In the Philistines, and in Saul, the prince of the power of the air was at work (*Eph.* 2:2). But God, who is over all, directed and disposed of these evil actions so that they furthered his ends, and thus they failed to destroy the righteous.

A farmer may have an artesian well spring up on his property, threatening to flood or erode his precious soil. However, it is possible to redirect the water so as to serve his ends rather than to injure his fruitful land. So God, who is not the author of sin, makes the works of the devil and his willing agents serve rather than injure his own good and righteous kingdom.

Saul meant evil against David, but in the very same events God meant it for good (*Gen.* 50:20). Saul's persecution drove David into wider contact with the people of Judah. It enlarged David's hunt for justice. It provided a small community in which David learned to govern by principle, and through which he laid foundation blocks for the nation of Israel.

Although no glory or apparent strength was yet attached to it, a completely new kingdom was being established for God's people. Samuel had anointed a young son of Jesse to be the next king of Israel. Divine blessing on the youth's military exploits in the name of the Lord and on behalf of the Lord's people gave him national prominence. A corps of young, brave men was living with the new king in exile.

Here they lived the early chapters of romantic exploits with God's chosen shepherd of Israel. In the wilderness they forged their loyalty to a dashing leader; they learned of his integrity; they came instinctively to understand his mind. They would be chief officers and administrators of the new kingdom.

While Saul was obsessed with killing the one who threatened his dynasty, and was thus distracted from the duties of his office, David was engaged in much more than self-defence. God was developing within the anointed, but not yet reigning, youth a devotion to justice for God's people. By the term 'justice', the Old Testament has in view, not so much the proceedings of a court, as the characteristic of using one's strength to support and defend the weak, the disadvantaged, and the oppressed.

David directed his band to honour and serve the small towns and the exposed shepherds of the territory in which they operated. It was common for farmers and villages to face incursions of armed Philistine marauders at harvest time, to have their crops and homes plundered. Upon hearing of such news in southern Judah, David and his men would fly to the relief of their fellow-citizens. Shepherds, alone in the search for scarce grasslands and still waters, would encounter meandering Bedouins, who would not scruple to help themselves to the caretaker's flock. David's army became a shield to shepherds, and the defenders of the helpless.

In David there grew a compassion for the helpless. To David's men came increased discipline and direction to noble causes. God's providence drove them to extremities in which they found new realms of service. Attention was diverted away from licking their personal wounds or nursing grudges.

2. Saving Providence

This was a time when David and his six hundred moved from one place in the wilderness to another, running from Saul's pursuit, hiding from expected assault. It is not clear that David recognized then how all this adversity was fashioning within him and his men a superior character that would better serve God's kingdom in the future. However, David was conscious, from day to day, of the protective care of divine providence. His Psalms are filled with acknowledgment of the Lord's hand in his many narrow escapes.

We find many evidences of God's providence limiting Saul's all-consuming attempt to kill David. In the wilderness of Ziph, 'Saul sought him every day, but God did not give him into his hand' (*1 Sam.* 23:14). The frustrated king could not find David. Saul even brought Jonathan along for the hunt. Slipping away from his father's encampment, 'Jonathan ... went to David at Horesh, and strengthened his hand in God' (*1 Sam.* 23:16). Remarkably, Jonathan said to his friend, 'Do not fear, for the hand of Saul my father shall not find you. You shall be king over Israel, and I shall be next to you. Saul my father also knows this' (*1 Sam.* 23:17). Thus Saul's pursuit served to encourage David to hope. Once, in the Wilderness of Maon, Saul's troops were actually encircling David and his men. At that instant an urgent message arrived of a Philistine invasion, forcing Saul to abort his mission.

After Saul and his army had chased the Philistines from the land, the king and a troop of three thousand immediately returned to the chase of David. No longer was his prey in the Wilderness of Maon, where he had come within an eyelash of capturing his son-in-law. The man-hunt took Saul to Engedi. Again in mountainous territory, Saul's forces had no immediate signs of David's tracks.

On this occasion, divine providence placed Saul within the immediate grasp of David and his mightiest warriors. Saul entered a cave to relieve himself, leaving his soldiers to watch the entrance. Nonetheless, David and his men were already inside this very cavern. David graciously spared Saul's life and shamed him into cutting short this expedition. David recognized that it was not chance, nor luck, nor his own skills of evasion which saved him from so many 'close calls'. The Lord had been watching over him and had delivered him from danger.

3. Reading the Future by Providence

Many who lived during David's era were quite aware that the Almighty manages all things on the earth and all things in human affairs. In David's time it was as it is today. Those who have a doctrine of divine providence often attempt to read divine intent for the future through unfolding circumstances, all of which are under God's control, or through opportunities set before them by the Lord's governing of our world.

When Keilah fell under attack from the Philistines, David's men feared that responding to help the people of that city would provide Saul with a golden opportunity to capture David and his small band. Since Keilah was so close to the border of Philistia, and therefore, since it faced constant raids from Israel's arch-foe, the city had built defensive walls. If David and his men entered a walled city, so they reasoned, they would be trapped. Saul would then hasten from Gibeah and seize them all. It was for this reason that David's army preferred to remain in the open wilderness where numerous routes of escape were their protection. Providence dictated, it seemed to them, that they decline to help Keilah.

David reasoned differently and inquired of the Lord as to what his will was (*1 Sam*. 23:2–5). Through Gad the prophet, and through the Urim and Thummim in Abiathar's possession, David could entreat God and hear his word in response. Thus did David rise above guesses as to God's intentions from the mere observation of providence. For him, prayer and 'Thus saith the Lord' would guide all decisions. So must we seek to know God's will by prayer and by the searching of his Word as we make decisions for the future.

After David and his forces delivered Keilah from the Philistines, Saul indeed did hear that the brave men of Jesse's son were in the fortress of Keilah. Reading providence only, Saul concluded, 'God has given him into my hand, for he has shut himself in by entering a town that has gates and bars' (*1 Sam.* 23:7). Not unaware of their danger, and employing informers, David knew when 'Saul summoned all the people to war, to go down to Keilah, to besiege David and his men' (*1 Sam.* 23:8). Again he sought by prayer and by inquiring of God to know what he should do. God told him that Saul was on his way. He further told David that, in the face of overwhelming numbers, and in the face of their rightful king's demand, Keilah's elders would deliver David and his men into Saul's hand. Then, and only then, did David and his men depart in haste.

As we have seen, when David was in the region of Engedi (*1 Sam.* 24), Saul entered a cave, unaware that David and his men were hidden in this very cavern. David's men, reading the providence of God, said, 'Here is the day of which the LORD said to you, "Behold, I will give your enemy into your hand"' (*1 Sam.* 24:4). The opportunity was there to kill Saul and to seize the kingdom after the assassination. How many presume that God wants us to act in a certain way because there is an unexpected opportunity to do so!

David did not need Gad, nor did he need the Urim and Thummim, to tell him what God's will was. He knew, as well as we, that, 'the governing authorities ... that exist have been instituted by God' (*Rom.* 13:1). He spoke of their advice as bad counsel, 'to put out my hand against him, seeing he is the LORD's anointed' (*1 Sam.* 24:7). On principle, received from the Word of God, he refused to seize his 'opportunity' against Saul.

How often are we met with flippant comments like, 'The Lord showed me', or, 'I was led of the Lord'! Often, by these slogans men and women mean, 'I have glanced at providence; I have read circumstances through the lenses of my personal optimism or pessimism, and with my personal wishes near at hand.' It is possible to use the above phrases if by them we mean, 'I have prayed for God's guidance and I have found these principles in his Word which give light to my path.'

Providence does inform us of God's having acted in the past. It is far less yielding of information about the future will of God. If God's Word informs us of God's ways, how much we can see of his hand at work in our own lives! How many praises we should give for surprising deliverances and unexpected grace! We should sharpen our sensitivity to our God's omnipresence. One of its major evidences is his control and meaningful direction in every circumstance of our lives.

11

IN THE WILDERNESS–3: CONSCIENCE

1 Samuel 24

In 1 Samuel 26:20, David's description of his situation to Saul was, 'The king of Israel has come out to seek a single flea like one who hunts a partridge in the mountains.' David, the partridge, took refuge in the mountains and caves of southern Judah. In 1 Samuel 24 we have an account of him and his men during their time in the region of Engedi, near the western shore of the Dead Sea. David's six hundred men were scattered in the hills of the region to evade Saul's force of three thousand.

We have already referred to the incident described in this chapter. Saul was travelling by the entrance of the very cave which held David and his men. The king, needing to relieve himself, entered the cave alone. Once inside, he took off his outer robe, a symbol of royal dignity. After laying his garment on a rock, he went a bit deeper into the cave to follow the call of nature. David and his men were observing this from a dark recess of the cave. The young warrior's lieutenants felt a surge of excitement. They argued to their leader that God had given David's enemy into his hands. Rather than slaying Saul, as he could easily have done, David cut a piece from Saul's prestigious robe. Allowing the king to exit the cave, David publicly confronted him from the mouth of the cave. There, David pleaded the injustice of Saul in seeking his life and he displayed the evidence that he had just then spared his monarch's life.

1. The Human Conscience

In this dramatic event of history we are given insight into a sharp contrast in two men's consciences. Conscience is a most vital element of the human soul. Being made in the image of God requires an awareness of righteousness and sin. From the beginning God etched upon every human soul the moral law which reflects the Lord's righteous character. Romans 2:14–15 tells us that even those who have never seen nor heard the Ten Commandments have within themselves a divine work, namely a divine writing in their hearts of the requirements of this very law. It is this moral law which accounts for the human instinct to reflect on one's own words and actions and, in this self-reflection, make a moral self-evaluation. Men and women accuse themselves or excuse themselves. From conscience come feelings of guilt, fear, and shame on the one hand or feelings of innocence, peace, and unabashed openness on the other.

Sigmund Freud taught that no moral law of God exists, but only a human awareness of society's expectations. To him the evil culprit disturbing man's mental peace is the *superego,* or conscience. His system of psychotherapy, which has prevailed for so long in the West, is, in reality, a determined attack upon the validity of conscience. By reconstructing men's consciences, Freud expected to eliminate aberrant behaviours which arise from guilt, fear, and shame, and are identified by him as the symptoms of 'insanity' and 'mental illness'. Such psychotherapeutic goals are doomed to failure because the conscience is a basic building block of man's being. Conscience may not be ripped out of man, unless to dehumanize him.

John Bunyan was correct in his book, *The Holy War.* When Diabolos captured Mansoul, he deposed old Mr Recorder (Conscience) as the town scribe and set up Forget-Good in his post. But even Diabolos could not slay old Recorder. The Devil drugged him to keep him quiet, but every once in a while Recorder roared most hideously and thereby terrified the entirety of Mansoul.

In the incident at Engedi during which Saul and David occupied the same cave, we see the enormous contrast between a good conscience and an evil one. We read that David had no sonner cut off a corner of Saul's robe than '[his] heart struck him' (*1 Sam.* 24:5). He openly confessed to his men, 'The LORD forbid that I should do this thing to my lord, the LORD's anointed.'

2. A Conscience Quickened by Grace

Because he meditated on God's Word, David's conscience had become razor sharp. One of the best marks of spirituality is the sensitivity of conscience, ever alert and ever speaking with one of the moral judgments of God. One of the clear signs of a well-ordered conscience is the ability to admit wrongdoing quickly. David did not protect some image of his own perfection before his men. He did not pretend to possess never-erring judgment. He could quickly say to others, 'I was mistaken' or 'I was sinful'. His passion to justify God discloses a genuine interest in holiness. It is the opposite of cover-up.

A second sign of a tender and healthy conscience is the feeling of deep shame and guilt over actions for which no one else would blame him. David's conviction and embarrassment over having cut Saul's robe was a mystery to his men. They were thinking that he should have spilled Saul's blood! They were of the opinion that putting Saul to death was a just repayment for Saul's murderous persecution. Do you ever feel overwhelmed by conscience for sins which no one else can see?

David's conscience convicted him for a sin against which the Western world has shamefully hardened its conscience. God made Saul David's master, as David had acknowledged in 1 Samuel 24:6. It was David's God-given duty to honour the king, not to diminish his prestige of office by the slightest action. What sins have Westerners heaped up in vilifying magistrates and rulers! The Holy Spirit, by the pen of Peter, commanded us all, 'Honour the emperor' (*1 Pet.* 2:17). Yet how many today think it is a privilege of democracy to 'despise authority' and to 'speak evil of dignitaries', while Peter calls such behaviour demonic, the characteristic of 'brute beasts made to be caught and destroyed' (*2 Pet.* 2:10–12, NKJV).

3. A Conscience Long Hardened by Sin

As David confronted Saul outside the cave which these two men had shared only moments earlier, he delineated the evil Saul had done in pursuing one who meant him no harm. Furthermore the young man professed his submission to the old king in the most humble language, and he produced proof of kind intentions toward the king.

Saul's pursuit of David was not the whim of a moment. It was a longstanding and determined policy. His heart was 'fully set to do evil' (*Eccles.* 8:11). He had 'become callous' and had given himself up to 'sensuality, greedy to practice every kind of impurity' (*Eph.* 4:19). A hardened shell had formed on Saul's conscience by his repeated choices.

David's sudden appearance and direct accusation before both loyal troops and enemies was used by God to awaken a conscience long drugged into quietness. We may say that the king had a fit of conscience. As conscience lit up the darkened sky of Saul's soul like a massive display of lightning, it caused a convulsion of his entire being. In the face of this sight of his own sinful ways, composure was shed in an instant. His spirit was compelled momentarily to respond in ways to which he had become unaccustomed.

This should serve as a warning to all who have laboured extensively and long at silencing the unpleasant sounds of conscience within. The conscience is not exterminated. It will speak within you again! As one who has attended many dying men and women, I can tell you that it is not uncommon for the dying to experience a time in which conscience parades before the mind many covered and forgotten sins of the past. At last, when in judgment, men stand before their Lawmaker and Judge, 'every mouth will be stopped' (*Rom.* 3:19, NKJV).

No doubt conscience will be alive and well at that moment, inducing such silence. And what if those who never repent and receive forgiveness of sins in Christ must live throughout eternity with a very active conscience? Will not that internal, spiritual implement of self-condemnation be a torment worse than a physical fire for the body? Is hell even possible for a creature *not* made in God's image?

In a flash Saul was in tears (*1 Sam.* 24:16). A confession of sin and guilt was forced from his soul as air is squeezed from the body by a blow to the solar plexus. 'You are more righteous than I, for you have repaid me good, whereas I have repaid you evil', he tells David (*1 Sam.* 24:17). He blurts out the reality of his situation and says, 'the LORD put me into your hands' (*1 Sam.* 24:18). He bears witness to David's righteousness! 'You did not kill me when the LORD put me into your hands. For if a man finds his enemy, will he let him go away safe?' (*1 Sam.* 24:18–19).

Also present in Saul's paroxysm of conscience is fear: 'And now, behold, I know that you shall surely be king, and that the kingdom of Israel shall be established in your hand' (*1 Sam.* 24:20). Therefore the king begged the most wanted man, while that very man was still in exile, to spare his family and his own name! (*1 Sam.* 24:21). Jonathan had been right. His father Saul did know deep down in his heart that he would never capture David but that David would be king. Thus we have the fugitive attempting to comfort the mighty, but now tearful and blubbering, monarch with promises (*1 Sam.* 24:22).

Freud was correct in one thing. Conscience can bring manhood to its knees in an instant! Everyone watching this scene had to be amazed at the strangeness of the king's words and behaviour. Conscience is capable of producing 'insane' babblings and erratic behaviour. But the famed psychoanalyst sided with the wicked passions against conscience, the great witness to divine righteousness and justice which God has indelibly written upon the heart. What a dreadful error!

What Saul needed for the obtaining of a healthy mind was the renouncing of his ways of rebellion and a turning to God with full purpose of and endeavour after new obedience (see *Westminster Shorter Catechism*, Q. & A. 87). This would have set him in his right mind. However, this scene, despite all the tears of sorrow and admission of sin, was no such conversion. The ruler's conscience was pointing him in that direction, almost hauling him by his neck to that path, but he would not follow. What a terrible, soul-destroying tragedy!

David had learned by bitter experience how many times the conscience roared within Saul, only to have the king of Israel drug the conscience into yet another silent stupor. 'Then Saul went home, but David and his men went up to the stronghold' in the wilderness (*1 Sam.* 24:22). Saul would seek David's life again before many days had passed.

From childhood we have all sinned. At times the sin was done with no other human being as a witness. Even when no human voice has accused us, there has been the echo of God's law condemning us from deep within our souls. There has come a portent of the omniscient Judge of all the earth, who is frowning upon our thoughts, our idle words, and our secret deeds. At times our emotions have been shaken by this inner voice of conscience.

Also from youth we have practised 'getting hold of ourselves' when we are unnerved by conscience. We have sought out many devices to wipe our memories clean of guilt, fear, and shame. This process is called 'hardening our hearts'.

The voice of self-reproach is painful, but it calls to us to turn from our wicked ways and to seek forgiveness of sins. It calls us to search for a mediator and substitute who will satisfy divine justice for our breaches of the law. Although conscience does not name him, it is preparing us to look to Jesus for pardon and cleansing. There is no other to quiet conscience, while we squarely face our sins.

It was David, who instructed us, 'Today, if you hear his voice, do not harden your hearts' (*Psa.* 95:7–8). It was David's Son and David's Lord who said, 'Come to me, all who labour and are heavy laden, and I *will* give you rest' (*Matt.* 11:28). Conscience unrelieved is a *heavy* burden. Yet conscience is a friend to hurry you into the arms of the only Saviour from the broken law and its curse. As the world's psychology recognizes, dealing with conscience is at the centre of mental health.

12

IN THE WILDERNESS–4: VENGEANCE AND FORGIVENESS

1 Samuel 25

Six hundred warriors and their camp dependants are not easily hidden, even in the rugged hills of southern Judah. David and his army were constantly on the move in search of safety and provisions. For a time the 'outlaws' settled near Carmel. There are two Carmels in Israel. One is north and west of Galilee near the Mediterranean Sea. That Carmel is the site where Elijah confronted the prophets of Baal. The less-known Carmel, where David and his band settled, was in southern Judah, about midway along the length of the Dead Sea's western side.

In that region David encountered Nabal, a wealthy descendant of Caleb. Much of Nabal's wealth was invested in large flocks of sheep and goats. David and his armed men were 'a wall' to Nabal's herdsmen night and day (*1 Sam.* 25:16). As they stood watch against Saul's searches, they provided protection against thieves and predators for all who lived in the region. David's forces operated with strict discipline, never stealing from or plundering those whom David would one day rule.

1. Insults from Unexpected Sources

Sheep-shearing is much like harvest time. It is a season of hard work followed by celebration. Then note is taken of the annual increase of flocks, and profits from wool are calculated. Owners of flocks would send gifts to the poor and to those whose services advanced their prosperity. Any local ruler or strong man would send greetings to the farmer at shearing time and courteously remind him of protection provided to his herdsmen throughout the year.

David sent young men to Nabal at his time of sheep-shearing. They were instructed to speak with benedictions and with modest claims. Nabal well knew that David was the military hero of Israel. He knew also that David's presence as a warlord increased the ease and productivity of his farming enterprise. Yet Nabal insulted David with harsh accusations of rebellion against Saul. He sent away David's emissaries empty-handed, and with his rude comments ringing in their ears.

When the young men reported that Nabal had heaped scorn upon David, the anger of the son of Jesse flared up. Immediately David ordered four hundred troops to gird on their swords and ride to Nabal's encampment. We must note that he, who for so long had been self-controlled in the face of Saul's outrageous injustices, was now in the grip of fury brought on by hearing the words of Nabal. He, who sought the will of God so carefully in most exploits, followed sudden passions at another moment. Vengeance! David fully intended to return evil for personal injury.

Observe that Satan made his temptation thrust at David's greatest strengths of character, in which he had long excelled others in sanctification. It is as though the wily old serpent takes special delight in overcoming the strongest wall of the fortress round our hearts. This has often been the strategy of the wicked one. Moses was 'very meek, more than all people who were on the face of the earth' in his day (*Num.* 12:3). Yet what sin kept him from the land of promise? An outburst of rage against the people he led! Peter was a courageous defender of Jesus Christ, who took up a sword against a more numerous band of armed men. Yet he melted in cowardice on the same night when gently questioned by a servant girl! In just the same contradictory manner revenge flashed in the eyes of longsuffering David.

It is not that revenge itself is evil. Both Old Testament and New teach that vengeance is the prerogative of the Judge of all the earth: 'Vengeance is mine, I will repay, says the Lord' (*Rom.* 12:19, citing *Deut.* 32:35). Nor is it improper for rulers whom God has appointed in this world to act as God's agents in taking vengeance (*Rom.* 13:4). Yet Scripture forbids the individual from engaging in personal vengeance, however great his powers may be. 'Never avenge yourselves, but leave it to the wrath of God' (*Rom.* 12:19) is a principle of personal ethics, not of civil policy. Any confusion of these two applications damages social order.

2. A Fair Example of Seeking Forgiveness

While David took up his sword, another scene was being played out elsewhere. A young herdsman of Nabal had witnessed and heard his master's expressions of contempt for David. Recognizing the danger into which this affront brought the entire family, he hurried to the wisest head in the family, that of Abigail. In wisdom Nabal's wife quickly settled on a scheme to conciliate David.

There is high drama in the biblical account. Abigail intercepted David and his four hundred armed warriors just as the captain uttered a reckless oath to exterminate every male in Nabal's household (*1 Sam.* 25:21–22). Abigail saved her family and all the males on the estate from destruction; she also kept David from sinning by asking and receiving forgiveness. Her knowledge of how to seek forgiveness demonstrates deep wisdom, sadly, a wisdom deeper than that which is apparent in many modern churches.

Abigail humbled herself before the offended party (*1 Sam.* 25:23–24). She did not act arrogantly, as do some modern Christians who approach the offended by making demands of them. Today it is not uncommon to hear, 'I have asked God to forgive me for my sin against you, and he has forgiven me. Therefore you must forgive me also.' Often such claims are supported by the authority of churches, who demand that the injured party forgive the offender. Job's friends were led not to expect God's forgiveness until Job, whom they had offended, prayed for them (*Job* 42:8).

Abigail admitted her own guilt and that of her husband (*1 Sam.* 25:24–25). The two are one, which she saw clearly, though she herself had never voiced an insult. Again, how watered down are many modern notions regarding the seeking and receiving of forgiveness. How many Christian leaders today mistakenly advocate forgiving major offences, although the one who does serious injury never even confesses wrongdoing!

Other offenders provide lame confessions such as, 'I'm sorry if my words offended you.' Such 'confessions' manifest no real repentance, and, in fact, lay the burden of guilt on the offended one, who is made to appear much too sensitive. David was right to take offence; therefore Abigail admits guilt.

Nabal's wife made abundant restitution in two ways. First she gave David's men a larger gift than Nabal would have given even had he been properly grateful to them (*1 Sam.* 25:18, 27). Secondly she restored David's honour. Publicly he had been abused. Publicly therefore, before four hundred soldiers, she heaped upon him recognition of his greatness (*1 Sam.* 25:26–31). How often have we heard a mere, 'I'm sorry', which is supposed to repay all the damages done to another! This manifests no awareness that restitution is a biblical principle in both testaments. It never crossed the mind of Zacchaeus, for example, that he could repent of his sins and receive pardon without making amends to those whom he had cheated (*Luke* 19:8).

Only after her admission of guilt to the offended one, and after having made restitution, did Abigail request what she was seeking: 'Please forgive the trespass of your servant' (*1 Sam.* 25:28). She is a shining example of how to seek forgiveness.

It is to be said also that David is a shining example of one who grants forgiveness. 'Go up in peace to your house. See, I have obeyed your voice, and I have granted your petition' (*1 Sam.* 25:35). He vocalized his forgiveness; he accepted her apology. The matter was settled. There was peace between them.

3. Openness to Receive Warning

Into the midst of her humble apology Abigail wove a biblical view of taking personal vengeance. Since it was obvious that he was God's man who would sit on the throne of Israel, David would not want to have a guilty conscience for having spilled blood to settle a personal score, she reasoned. Nor would such a reputation enhance the honour which he had earned by winning the Lord's battles.

Her arguments were gently made, yet very direct. Abigail's speech illustrates Galatians 6:1: 'Brothers, if anyone is caught in any transgression, you who are spiritual should restore him in a spirit of gentleness.' And, yes, a woman may be the spiritual one to restore a man.

How appealing it is that David was not too chauvinistic to listen to the sound advice of a woman! With his male ego set on fire, the man of war nonetheless yielded to the spiritual advice of a wise woman. Unashamed of doing so even under the watching eyes of his troops, David praised God: 'Blessed be the LORD, the God of Israel, who sent you this day to meet me! Blessed be your discretion, and blessed be you, who have kept me this day from bloodguilt and from avenging myself with my own hand! . . . the LORD the God of Israel . . . has restrained me from hurting you' (*1 Sam.* 25:32–34). Do we make it a matter for praise when God prevents us from carrying out our evil intentions?

David openly confessed his sinful intent in the mission he was undertaking. This readiness to admit fault would later reappear as the prophet Nathan rebuked the king for sins that had been carried through. Most of us instinctively deny wrongdoing and seek to gloss over it. We seem to think that greatness lies in the appearance of sinlessness rather than in the genuine openness which owns our sins. David did not attempt to fulfil his evil and foolish oath. Men like Saul, who posture before other men to win their admiration, do attempt to keep unwise and sinful oaths. This Saul did when he tried to execute his own son for disobeying an order which Jonathan had never heard uttered.

On the next day Abigail reported to Nabal what David had been about to do, and how she had averted the disaster. Whether through wounded pride or terror at his near escape from a violent death, it appears that Nabal had a series of strokes and died within ten days. Upon hearing the news, David rejoiced that the Judge of all the earth had brought vengeance on wicked Nabal (*1 Sam.* 25:39). Some of God's vengeance is executed in this life. 'When the wicked perish there are shouts of gladness' (*Prov.* 11:10).

4. Tangled Affairs of the Heart

Immediately David took Abigail to be his wife. He also married Ahinoam. Saul had by this time multiplied his insults to David by giving his wife, Michal, to another man.

God tolerated polygamy in Old Testament times, when even the saints lacked the fullness of revelation and the fullness of the Spirit. However, in every record of polygamous homes, there are accounts of jealousies and conflicts. Thus we are shown that multiple marriages were never a part of the creation institution of marriage. The most profound miseries of David's life arose from the sin of polygamy. Never did this man of God find the peace in his home which God has always intended to be a blessing of marriage.

When David took Abigail to be his wife, we do not have a tale of young and innocent love. There are dark shadows of hardness of heart in both bride and groom. Lurking nearby on their wedding day is divine disapproval of polygamy. Yet there was an element to this union which in other circumstances would have been exemplary.

Their mutual attraction was in a nobility of character that they found in one another. For years Abigail had lived with an insolent, drunken, and evil-tongued rogue. In David she saw a man who served the Lord, who was approachable and guileless. David was drawn to a woman of grace and wisdom as well as of an uncommon beauty. Both understood how to confess guilt and how to grant pardon. These are important traits for making any marriage successful. Nonetheless, such a rationale should not override the commands of God.

13

IN THE WILDERNESS–5: THE FINAL ENCOUNTER

1 Samuel 26

History does have its repetitions. Once before (*1 Sam.* 23:19–20) David had hidden in the hill of Hachilah and the Ziphites had informed Saul about his location. Divine providence had prevented David from being surrounded by Saul's forces when the Philistines had invaded Israel, and the king had been summoned to defend the land. Now again (*1 Sam.* 26:1) David hid in Hachilah. Again the Ziphites informed on him. Again Saul and three thousand troops descended upon the region. Again divine providence delivered David, but divine providence has an infinite variety of instruments for accomplishing its purposes.

1. Vigilance and Sleep

David and Saul at this point met and talked for the last time in their lives. Nothing had changed with the parties to this drama. David had gained all the friends he was to have. Enemies against David were resolved in their enmity. The living and true God still kept David under the cruellest persecution. Yet slight changes suggest movement.

David did not presume upon friendly providence. His watchfulness had become more intense. The pursued had sent out spies before Saul was near to his camp. Advance sentinels gave him early and accurate intelligence. There would be no near-entrapment this time. David was now in command of the territory, advancing at will into the heart of the enemy's camp.

With stealth, and owning the night, a dashing and bold raid took David to the very side of the sleeping monarch. Having arisen at night personally to survey the enemy camp, David had two warriors by his side. Unexpectedly, the hero of Israel asked for a volunteer to go with him to Saul in the camp. He was more aggressive than ever in this war of nerves with the king.

Abishai readily offered to go with David. He was a man of adventure! He was of David's thirty most heroic men. Once he had single-handedly slain three hundred men with a spear. Abishai was David's nephew, son of Zeruiah (David's older half-sister) and brother of Joab. With numerous exploits David and Abishai had honed their daring to a razor-sharp edge. They were about to launch one of their most thrilling enterprises.

As the two audacious men of valour began to creep into the encamped army of three thousand, they discovered that all the sentinels were asleep. They arrived at the centre of the temporary fortress to find the king's bodyguard also in a sound sleep. Abner, Saul's uncle and captain of the royal guard, was asleep near the king. 'They were all asleep, because a deep sleep from the LORD had fallen upon them' (*1 Sam.* 26:12).

While the entire camp slept, David and Abishai had a conversation, during which they stood next to the king and the captain of the royal guard! Abishai opened the discussion with a request for permission to kill Saul with the king's own spear, thrust into the ground at the head of the sleeping ruler. After all, Abishai reasoned, God's providence had delivered David's enemy into his hand. He reasoned that it was obviously God's will that his murderous enemy die.

David answered with reasons from the Word of God. He ordered Abishai not to kill Saul. No one may slay God's anointed and be guiltless. God will strike Saul with disease or accident, or Saul may die a natural death, or he may die in battle, but 'the LORD forbid that I should put out my hand against the LORD's anointed' (*1 Sam.* 26:11). Instead, David took Saul's spear and water jar. The two men made their escape with no one having noticed them.

Perhaps the sleep was all supernaturally induced. But perhaps there was already a heaviness of spirit in Saul and his warriors. They had been vainly chasing David and his six hundred men throughout the wilderness of Judah. Yet Saul kept pressing on with a sinful pursuit that never brought satisfaction. 'The way of the treacherous is their ruin' (*Prov.* 13:15). While under a bondage to keep on a wicked path, sinners grow weary. Faculties begin to sleep when under the direction of a heart hardened by lusts. Tragically, spiritual stirrings have become by now dim and distant memories.

Scripture cries to men who are sold under sin, 'Awake, O sleeper, and arise from the dead, and Christ will shine on you' (*Eph*. 5:14). Saul appeared to be stumbling through the motions of seeking David, and through the forms of apologizing to David.

However, there was less emotion and less energy in every step and every word. This would be his last meeting with David, his last opportunity to repent. The day of death was nearer than Saul expected! After that, the dreadful reality of judgment!

Persistent sinners should not presume on the providence of God. No one who walks in rebellion may expect a trumpet blast to awaken him when death and judgment are near. Often God puts to sleep those who have sinned against conscience and against past warnings. Then he rolls them sleeping into eternity, where hell fires await them. They waken to find that weapons and water are no longer available to assist their souls.

While sinners sleep with drugged consciences giving no alarm, with voices of rebuke silenced, what enemies of their souls relieve them quietly of their most needed supplies! Once they had sinned with every sense of the body fearing reprisal, tense with readiness to flee danger. But that was so long ago. Now the reflexes are dull and unresponsive. 'Therefore stay awake—for you do not know when the master of the house will come' (*Mark* 13:35).

2. Forgiveness and Trust

Standing at a safe distance from the dreaded army, David called out to Saul's forces. As he wakened the camp, he did so by berating Abner, who had been charged with protecting the king, yet Abner had slept at his post. In many armies martial law allows for the punishment of sleeping sentries with death. 'As the LORD lives, you deserve to die, because you have not kept watch over your lord, the LORD's anointed. And now see where the king's spear is and the jar of water that was at his head' (*1 Sam.* 26:16). Trophies of the night's exploit were held high for all to observe.

By this time Saul was aroused. He was the first to recognize David's voice. 'Is this your voice, my son David?' Now the son of Jesse began to ignore the humiliated Abner. Instead of addressing him he made an impassioned plea that there was no cause for the king to hunt him down. David argued his own insignificance: Would a mighty ruler dispatch his armies to find a mere flea? Would a great hunter criss-cross an entire mountain to find one partridge which had flown there to escape? It was a mad business to expend so much energy for one who was nothing of note!

Even then Saul's servant would not place the blame on the king. Perhaps the Lord had stirred up Saul's heart to pursue David, he reasoned. Or some other men may have incited the king to seek his life. If it had been the Lord, an offering should placate him. If it had been men, and if they had been at fault, let the Lord curse them. No curses fell on Saul from the lips of David.

In the midst of his plea David exposed the way in which the banishment had caused him the most pain of heart. If men had incited the king, 'they have driven me out this day that I should have no share in the heritage of the LORD, saying, "Go, serve other gods."' Prolonged absence from civilized Israel had denied David access to the worship of the Most High at the tabernacle and among the prophets.

The great inheritance of the Jews was Mosaic worship through their priests and prophets. 'How lovely is your dwelling place, O LORD of hosts! My soul longs, yes, faints for the courts of the LORD; my heart and flesh sing for joy to the living God' (*Psa.* 84:1–2).

Being driven from the only centres of true worship on earth was a sentence which meant that one was only exposed to the worship of other gods. In this sentence flows the deepest reality of David's soul, the anguish of banishment from soul-satisfying worship of the living God. How he loved the real treasure of Israel more than silver, gold or power! Have you such high regard for spiritual worship of the God of all the earth? Appropriate biblical worship is no little treasure. Those who tamper with it and take it away are robbing the saints of their inheritance.

David had just spared the king's life again, when it was under his power. David respectfully professed loyalty to the Lord's anointed. He asked what he had done to provoke Saul's pursuit. 'Behold, as your life was precious this day in my sight, so may my life be precious in the sight of the LORD, and may he deliver me out of all tribulation'

(*1 Sam.* 26:24). Saul responded with confession of sin. 'I have sinned . . . Behold, I have acted foolishly, and have made a great mistake' (*1 Sam.* 26:21). Saul promised a change of mind and behaviour. 'I will no more do you harm.'

He invited David back into his former relationships at Gibeah and with Saul's household and army. 'Return, my son David.' The king was saying, 'I repent, so let's go back to how things used to be.' Verbally, Saul said everything he should have done to repent.

David could not see into the king's heart to know the sincerity of his statements. However, there had been years of mental and spiritual instability in Saul. There had been many professions of repentance, only to be followed quickly by his seeking David's life once more. David had had a long history of being seriously injured by Saul. He did not trust the king's words, although he did not say so. After Saul's expression of confession and repentance, David cautiously offered to return the monarch's spear. But no seasoned warrior was to approach David. A single young man must come to David to recover this trophy. David thus displayed that he did not trust Saul. Following the invitation to return, 'David went his way, and Saul returned to his place' (*1 Sam.* 26:25).

There was no trust. Very soon thereafter David in his heart thought, 'Now I shall perish one day by the hand of Saul' (*1 Sam.* 27:1). Trust had not been restored. David's only trust was in the Lord.

In Luke 17:3–4, Jesus taught, 'If your brother sins, rebuke him, and if he repents, forgive him, and if he sins against you seven times in the day, and turns to you seven times, saying, "I repent", you must forgive him.'

Readiness to forgive those who say, 'I repent', is a duty. To put the matter behind one's back and to seek no further judicial recourse for an injury from that moment is required of those who forgive. However, the repair of trust when broken is not so easily accomplished. Nor is it required that anyone expose himself to further injury after he has been seriously and repeatedly hurt by the hands of one who has shown himself 'unstable'.

Churches and Christian counsellors go too far when they insist that forgiveness requires returning to former relationships as though nothing has broken them. Forgiveness does not require the injured to risk more of the same mistreatment in friendship, marriage, or business. In these days we hear of too many unwise pressures which are brought upon injured parties in the name of forgiveness. There may come a time when men must go separate ways: 'David went his way, and Saul returned to his place.'

14

EXILE

1 Samuel 27:1–28:2; 29:1–30:6

In David's final encounter with Saul, God had remarkably blessed the young warrior with success in a bold exploit. The Lord God of Israel had defeated the king's attempt to seize David and had humbled the now wicked ruler before his younger, newly anointed one. No one could doubt that the Lord was with the son of Jesse.

1. Depression

Human emotions are reactive. It is not uncommon to experience despondency soon after being filled with a thrill of triumph. As this occurred within David, we are given insight into the thoughts of his heart: 'Now I shall perish one day by the hand of Saul. There is nothing better for me than that I should escape to the land of the Philistines. Then ... I shall escape out of his hand' (*1 Sam.* 27:1).

Strange fads develop among the writers of commentaries. One follows another's opinion about a section of

Scripture until every voice holds the same view. It has been common to view the exile of David among the Philistines as a period of sin and spiritual decline, although the Word of God makes no such accusation.

Many detect in David's despondency a lack of trust in God. However, it is not uncommon to feel despair after having been subjected to vicious abuse for years. It was realistic for David to expect Saul's swift return to hunting for his son-in-law. Though the confrontation on the hill of Hachilah had been a moral victory for him, David realized, nonetheless, that nothing had really changed.

By now Saul knew as well as David the places where six hundred men could be concealed in southern Judah. Scouts of the ruler could be dispatched to each of these locations. In earlier days, when David and his men were a young band of fugitives, they could make midnight escapes or climb over the rugged rocky ridges like mountain goats. They could spend many days in vigorous action without food and with little water. Now they were responsible for wives and children, who could not be so easily moved and who could not so easily face deprivation. Tied down as they were to heavier responsibilities, it became increasingly unlikely that his band could continue avoiding Saul.

This situation reminds us that one must be careful when attempting to help disheartened saints. When believers are discouraged, they do need encouragement to trust in the Lord and in his promises. However, it is no help to adopt a theory that to be downhearted is sin. Nor is it accurate. The saints often face dismal prospects. Their negative assessments may be quite correct. Refusal to flee for safety is not necessarily an act of faith. Quickness to accuse the dispirited of sin creates serious complications for those who have good reasons, circumstantial or physical, to be dejected. Rebuke is not a helpful remedy for the disconsolate.

2. *Self-Banishment*

A solution to the constant and growing danger from the ravings of Saul occurred to David. He had once before used this device successfully in providing protection for his parents (*1 Sam.* 22:3).

David and his entire retinue would become expatriates among the Philistines. This scheme succeeded. 'And when it was told Saul that David had fled to Gath, he no longer sought him' (*1 Sam.* 27:4).

Commentators seize upon the fact that Scripture does not mention David's enquiring of the Lord in making this decision. Based upon this silence they accuse David of prayerlessness and of being far from God. Enquiring of God by prophets or by Urim and Thummim was apparently a practice reserved for times of national emergency. But this decision was not made in such an hour. A great case has been built on the silence of Scripture as to David's praying at this time. It is not an impressive case. Rulers are expected to be decisive without direct revelation.

David and his band sought refuge with Achish, ruler of Gath. There is disagreement as to whether this was the same Achish whom David had met before (*1 Sam.* 21:10–15). The Israelite company was welcomed to live in Gath by the arch-enemies of Israel. This is a seeming contradiction, but it is a situation often experienced by Christians. Believers many times find greater civility and kindness from the world then they do from the church. What a tragedy it is when brethren do not dwell together in unity, and the only respite on earth for the people of God is with the heathen!

Living under the watchful eye of Achish would prove not to be convenient for long. After demonstrating that his people would be loyal and law-abiding citizens under Achish, David asked the Philistine whether he might be granted a city to manage for him. Achish gave the refugees Ziklag, on the southwestern border of Judah and far from his own capital. From there David would conduct military missions. Yet he would visit Gath often and give Achish a portion of his spoils of war. Achish was well pleased with his new subject. By the end of David's sixteen-month sojourn (*1 Sam.* 27:7), Achish would say of him, 'I have found nothing wrong in you from the day of your coming to me to this day. . . . you are as blameless in my sight as an angel of God' (*1 Sam.* 29:6, 9).

3. Advancing God's Kingdom in Israel

David was no fool. He never imagined that he could bare all of his heart to Achish. The exile never shared his intent to further the welfare of Israel, even while in Philistia. Nor was David ignorant of the possibility of compromising situations arising.

He had no doubt thought through his own purposes and what his behaviour would be if war came between

Israel and Achish. He knew that it would take great sagacity to pull off his plans.

Again commentators cite David's failure to tell all to Achish as a sign of his having fallen into great sin. He who does not choose carefully to whom he will share all that is in his heart and mind, however, is surely acting like a child. There is much information which we withhold even from trusted friends. How much more from enemies! The tongues of the Israelites had to be carefully guarded in order for them to secure safety among the Philistines. What is amazing is that David exercised such incredible discipline over more than six hundred tongues, including those of men, women, and children!

From Ziklag the Davidic army raided the Geshurites, Girzites, and Amalekites. These tribes were long-time enemies of Israel who constantly destabilized the south of Judah. They were among the peoples under a divine sentence of rejection dating from the days of Joshua. Their extermination had been commanded by Moses and Joshua.

These foes were eliminated by the assaults of the Ziklag Brigade. Plunder from them filled Achish's coffers. He was satisfied with David's general reports about the Judean regions in which his troops operated. He assumed that David was harming Jews and making enemies of his own countrymen. David was pleased with Achish's conclusions and did not inform him of the truth, which was that he was actually strengthening Judah!

Commentators accuse David of great sin because he did not fight according to the Geneva Convention. No one did in that time. Few do in the Middle East to this day. God had commanded genocide to heathen, idolatrous tribes whose time of iniquity was full, and who lived in the land where the Jews must be kept from the transgressions of the godless. These extreme measures were chosen so that God's promise of Messiah's coming might be fulfilled.

1 Chronicles 12 also reports that, during this period, a great number of warriors from Israel defected to David at Ziklag. Many even came from Saul's own tribe of Benjamin. In this remote region David's army was growing ever larger. God was preparing David for the hour near at hand when Saul would be taken from Israel. These expanded forces could not have been hidden in the crevices of the Judean deserts and forests. God's providence was wondrously at work in making David the outlaw into David the mighty king.

The inevitable hour arrived! Achish summoned David to march with him and with all the Philistine princes against Saul and Israel. There was to be a massive invasion. David's growing number of men marched with Achish. We know that on many occasions David had risked his life and the welfare of his troops by refusing to lift his hand against the Lord's anointed. Who could doubt that in his mind plans were being conceived to make his forces useful to Israel's defence rather than to joining in the assault? Perhaps his men had already been informed of these intentions in their own council of war.

Although Achish trusted David, the other Philistine princes realized the truth. They were angry with Achish.

'What are these Hebrews doing here?' (*1 Sam.* 29:3). 'He shall not go down with us to battle, lest in the battle he become an adversary to us' (verse 4). In typical Eastern conversation Achish exaggerated his fondness of David. In expected Eastern style, David objected to being excluded from the battle. Perhaps he genuinely regretted having no opportunity to fight the Philistines in saving Israel. This too was God's providence. It was to be the day of Saul's death in battle by divine appointment.

David's Lord had blessed his servant's decision to live among the Philistines. There was temporary peace for the people under his command. There was success in strengthening Judah. Increased prosperity and numerical growth came to David and his men. The favour of his host prince was secure. And the Lord had delivered the Hebrews from dangerous places in the midst of the Philistine army. One can hardly judge this period of David's life as that of a prodigal or backslidden believer, as most seem prone to do.

It had been about a fifty-mile march for David's men, first from Ziklag to Gath, where they had met Achish, and then on to Aphek, where all the troops of the Philistine princes were assembling for war against Israel. After being dismissed, the Hebrew contingent had to retrace its steps. A shocking calamity awaited the tired army at their homes.

Ziklag had been burned with fire. There were no corpses, but all their wives and children were gone as were all their earthly goods. While David's troops marched with Achish, Amalekites, whom they had provoked with earlier raids, took revenge on their Jewish enemies: captivity for their families, plunder of their possessions, and destruction of their homes.

All of the men of war 'raised their voices and wept until they had no more strength to weep' (*1 Sam*. 30:4). These men, who had shared so many dangers and so many thrills of victory, now shared together the bitter cup of disaster.

David had received them into his band when each fled the reign of Saul into the wilderness of Judah. He had led them for years through many dangers and many exciting military exploits. But now, at this sign of their first serious setback, 'the people spoke of stoning him' (*1 Sam*. 30:6).

The son of Jesse had suffered the same losses as did they. However, in distress those who are suffering are all too prone to look for someone to blame. Leaders are the most visible targets. Subjects think that rulers should have foreseen and guarded against sudden assaults of war, plagues, or economic depressions. In the West, we want some leader to 'take responsibility'. Contempt and criticism rise quickly from fickle followers. Leadership is not a stable position to hold.

If David would be king, he must learn about capricious and impulsive subordinates. If God had given him favour with a Philistine prince, so too must he depend on God alone to keep him in the good graces of those whom he served most affectionately. The approval of any man can be a vain thing upon which to lean.

15

ASCENDING TO A THRONE

1 Samuel 28 & 31

David was to be king of Israel! For this Jesse's son had been anointed by Samuel at the direction of the Most High God. Oil had been poured on his head in his youth. There had intervened long years in the school of persecution for the prospective king. But now the hour designated by God for transition of power from Saul to David was near. In Jehovah's unsearchable wisdom it would be an hour of weakness for David. And it would be an hour of devastation and disgrace for the nation of Israel over which he came to rule.

1. The Humble Condition of Both David and Israel

It is a repeated theme in the symphony of God's providence that the Almighty resists the proud but gives grace to the humble of heart. 'He sets on high those who are lowly' (*Job* 5:11). The first word of his accession to the throne of Israel would reach David where he was hidden in a little city of Philistia, exiled from his fellow-countrymen. He would be sitting amidst the smouldering ashes of buildings that had been burned by Amalekite marauders. His followers had mutinied against him, only hours before having taken counsel to stone him. Their wives were trembling still from the terrifying captivity from which they had been delivered by the skin of their teeth. How strange it is to human reason that the Lord would take David to such a lowly experience, as the setting for the announcement that his time to be king had come!

As this scene was being divinely directed in Ziklag in southern Philistia, an even more destructive event was overtaking Israel, the nation which David was soon to rule. On the Plain of Jezreel the largest contingent of Philistine warriors ever to invade Israel during Saul's reign had set themselves in array. They had chosen the northern heights above the plain. Saul, having summoned all of Israel to this engagement, had prepared for battle at the southern edge of the plain on Gilboa (*1 Sam.* 28:4). When Saul had personally surveyed the massive army of the Philistines, 'he was afraid, and his heart trembled greatly' (*1 Sam.* 28:5).

Jezreel has soaked up the blood of numerous great armies who have met there from pre-Israelite to modern times. It is the site named in Revelation (whether symbolic or literal) for the gathering of the kings of the earth in the great day of the Lord (*Rev.* 16). When the battle was joined on the Plain of Jezreel at the close of Saul's reign, the blood of Israel was not spared. Saul and his three sons (including noble Jonathan) died in one day (*1 Sam.* 31:6). Then horror and panic struck the ranks of Israel's soldiers.

They fled. Not only did the Philistines loot the cities of the plain, they took control of those cities. Because Jezreel spreads all the way to the Jordan River, the Philistines crossed into Trans-Jordan and captured cities there as well. The nation of Israel was thoroughly trampled underfoot by the menace of Philistia. In such manner was the nation prepared for David's reign.

2. Witchcraft in High Places

What is more, Saul left an odour of the macabre upon Israel. The first king of Israel had been desired and chosen by the nation. Underlying their eagerness to have Saul rule over them was a distrust of the Lord's protective care. The strange last hours of Saul and the battle at Jezreel not only weakened Israel but also chastened them for trusting in princes and depending upon mere man for help. Is not modern man looking away from God to place confidence in princes?

Years before his death on the Plain of Jezreel, Saul had been sent by God on a mission to destroy the Amalekites. Very specific directions were disobeyed by the king. On that occasion Samuel had told the disobedient ruler that 'rebellion is as the sin of witchcraft' (*1 Sam.* 15:23, AV). Rejecting the Word of God is similar to idolatry. When one first encounters those comments of Samuel there can be an impulse to think that the prophet is using symbolic and poetic language to stress the evil of Saul's disobedience. However the eerie events at the close of Saul's life underscore the direct connection between disobedience to God's words and the practice of witchcraft. When nations turn from the Word of God, the occult emerges to take a prominent place in their societies.

When Saul, who was not usually cowardly in the face of combat, 'trembled greatly' at the massive Philistine forces (*1 Sam.* 28:5), the king 'inquired of the LORD' (*1 Sam.* 28:6). But long ago 'the Spirit of the LORD departed from Saul' (*1 Sam.* 16:14). Although he no longer had the benefit of having a prophet whom he could consult, Saul could still occasionally inquire through the Urim of the high priest, or he could privately pray for guidance to come by means of dreams. Yet because the king had no reverence for God's words, the Lord had ceased speaking to him.

At Jezreel, knowing that he faced overwhelming enemies, the king craved some word from supernatural sources. He desired a word of direction from someone who had knowledge of the future, some token of his receiving aid from higher powers. How often in modern times do we read of rulers who consult astrologers and those from various departments of the occult, with the hope of gaining some sort of knowledge that will enable them to face coming troubles.

Nations look to those in high offices as possessing superior wisdom and resources to lead them. But in moments of crisis, these who have made great promises in order to gain positions of 'power' know themselves to be mere men. When their kingdoms and their very lives are in the balance, there comes a consternation that makes them desperate to receive assistance from on high. If these leaders are not familiar with trusting the Word of God, and are not accustomed to visiting the throne-room of the Almighty in prayer to make their requests, they will visit the darkest dens of demonic presence for help. From trusting in the human frame alone, they are driven by panic to consult those who are held in chains, awaiting the judgment of the Almighty (*2 Pet.* 2:4; *Jude* 6).

Earlier in his reign Saul had done his best to exterminate spiritists, mediums, and witches from his kingdom. Now on the night before his death we have a chilling scene in which he goes in disguise to a witch at En-dor, ten miles distant from his camp at Gilboa. He asks her to conduct a séance for him. Superstitiously believing that she had access to the departed spirits of those who once walked the earth, he asks the witch to call up the spirit of Samuel from the realm of the dead so that he may speak with him.

3. The Occult Must Be Shunned

All false religions are a strange mixture of trickery and the real presence of evil spirits. Paul tells us in the New Testament that idols are nothing (*1 Cor.* 10:19)! Idols and all pertaining to their worship are mere material show with no spiritual reality. An idol is all wood, stone, metal, paper, etc. It is not to be feared or held in reverence.

But Paul goes on in 1 Corinthians 10:20 to say that Gentiles who worship idols sacrifice to demons. Idols have no spiritual or living reality. Yet demons linger near the places where idols are found. Satan and his legions of fallen spirits were never content to be creatures that would bring glory to God. Desiring to receive to themselves the honour and acclaim which the Father and the Son are given, they have led men into false religion.

Very early in the history of the world, Adam and Eve were tempted by Satan to trust their own wisdom and to disdain God's words. Having succeeded in his deceit, Satan and his demonic minions created false religions in human society. It is obvious that men will come to an end of human powers and will look round for aid. Then they may be entrapped in false religion. Although these sorry demons have no powers to assist humanity, and although they are not directly worshipped by men, they greedily take to themselves the honour men wrongly give to moon and stars, or to idols, honour which belongs to God alone.

In 1 Corinthians 12:2 Paul addresses Christians who once practised idolatry. He asks them to recall that in their idolatrous experience they were 'led astray' to mute idols by spiritual powers. Such forces moving them did not come from the idols but from the demons that were present. This point is made at the start of Paul's discussion of spiritual realities in worship. All spiritual forces are to be tested as to their validity by doctrine, not by our feelings or by a sense that these forces are 'leading' one in a certain direction. Those who practise false worship experience very real and powerful influences upon themselves. They are 'led' by evil spiritual beings.

For these reasons God warned through Moses in Deuteronomy 18:10–15:

> There shall not be found among you anyone who burns his son or his daughter as an offering, anyone who practices divination or tells fortunes or

> interprets omens, or a sorcerer or a charmer or a medium or a wizard or a necromancer, for whoever does these things is an abomination to the LORD. And because of these abominations the LORD your God is driving them out before you. You shall be blameless before the LORD your God, for these nations, which you are about to dispossess, listen to fortune-tellers and to diviners. But as for you, the LORD your God has not allowed you to do this. The LORD your God will raise up for you a prophet like me from among you, from your brothers—it is to him you shall listen.

When men reject the authority of God's prophet, they are but a short step away from witchcraft. Saints are to spurn all direction apart from God's Word. There is no entertainment in palm-reading, fortune-telling, séances, and witchcraft. With these we must have *nothing* to do. This reminder must be sounded in an age that is spawning literature about the occult. There is nonsense about 'white magic' and 'good witches' in books written for children, such as the *Harry Potter* series. It is to be found too in *The Lord of the Rings* and in *Star Wars*, where it is suggested that one can get in touch with mysterious powers and use them for good or for ill.

Saul went to a witch at night to speak with the dead. As she was conducting her clever deceits, the Lord actually sent the spirit of Samuel to her. None was more surprised at the actual presence of the prophet than she. She shrieked in terror at his appearance. Apparently Saul could see nothing, but the witch transmitted the message to the king.

Samuel confirmed to Saul that the Lord had become the king's enemy (*1 Sam.* 28:16). He indicated that Saul and his three sons would die the next day, the Philistines would triumph over his army, and David would become king (*1 Sam.* 28:17–19). Saul fell down full length on the ground in great terror. He had hoped for something other than the truth.

False religion is in the business of giving lying promises. But that weird séance was employed by the Sovereign of heaven and earth to give one last word from God to Saul. However, it was a word void of mercy.

Beware of departing from the living God. For the last day of his life, what darkness filled Saul's soul! He experienced the certainty of coming doom, the awareness that he was about to face God as an enemy, concern for his sons, sorrow for his nation, and regret for lost opportunities to repent.

As these agonies gripped Saul's inner man, he still had to go through the motions of one last battle. Tormented by hopelessness he died by an act of self-murder. To the last he worried more about falling into the hands of cruel men than into the hands of the living God.

16

LOOKING INTO THE FACE OF DEATH

2 Samuel 1

Such is the plight of fallen mankind that death strikes our awareness from all points of the compass. Even warriors must learn to process the catholic reality of death so as not to allow too intense a disturbance of their spirits. David had returned home only two days earlier from a battlefield slaughter of the Amalekites (*2 Sam.* 1:1). Now death extracted more visceral responses from him. News of the widespread devastation and death that had occurred in his own nation brought about a massive surging of his passions. The tragic demise of close friends required a vigorous engagement of mind, emotions, and will at the most profound depths of David's being.

A lone Amalekite wandered into Ziklag and prostrated himself at David's feet. His appearance bore all the external marks of a man in deep mourning, so as to signal the fact that he carried distressing news. Many Israelites were fallen dead at the hands of the Philistines, he told them. The remainder had fled from the enemy in panicked defeat. Saul, their king, and his noble son, Jonathan, had also died in the carnage.

1. Euthanasia

Seeing that his report had shocked the warlord of Ziklag, the Amalekite proceeded to enlarge upon his tale of war. What was to follow was partly true, partly fanciful and self-serving. But what is so fascinating in this account is the vast gulf between the world's attitudes toward death and those of a man who fears God. In the end the Amalekite would be the more shocked of the two men. It was incomprehensible to him that any intelligent man could hold David's view of death, and even act upon that view.

'By chance I happened to be on Mount Gilboa', he began. In fact, the battle had been building for days. None in the region could have been unaware of the tens of thousands of troops massing on each side. He had been no doubt determined to be one of the first to strip the dead for personal gain. 'And there was Saul', he went on, 'leaning on his spear . . .' (*2 Sam.* 1:6).

His tale was to the effect that Saul had been leaning on his spear in a failed suicide attempt. Yet the Philistine troops were almost upon him. Therefore, at Saul's request, this man had personally put the king out of his misery, for he could see that Saul would not live much longer in any case. Then the Amalekite had taken Saul's crown and armlet which he now brought to David (who would be the next king).

As he wove his story of euthanasia, an act which would, of course, issue in the advancement of David, the Amalekite clearly expected a handsome reward. After all, he had been merciful to the king, and he had done a great favour to David as well. Both the ancient and the modern world would be enthusiastic in commending him. It was (and is) common to think that relieving a human being of anguish by assisting him in dying is a commendable act. 'For the mind that is set on the flesh is hostile to God, for it does not submit to God's law; indeed, it cannot' (*Rom.* 8:7). Nor can such a mind even dream that anyone would reason differently. The thought is, 'Surely no one would follow the law in extreme emergencies like this!'

David's response, however, was to ask in disbelief, 'How is it you were not afraid to put out your hand to destroy the LORD's anointed?' (*2 Sam.* 1:14). Then he ordered the immediate execution of the messenger. Perhaps David realized that the man's account of Saul's death might be fictional. Whether it was or not, he had confessed to shedding the blood of God's servant as though that were a virtue. God is the Protector of those whom he appoints to office. Furthermore the command, 'You shall not murder' (*Exod.* 20:13), expresses the divine will regarding all who are made in his image. It is God's prerogative to give and to take away human life. An abiding divide stands between those who fear God and those who unjustly tamper with the lives of others.

David wrote in a Psalm, 'The transgression of the wicked saith within my heart, that there is no fear of God before his eyes' (*Psa.* 36:1, AV). When a society, whether in the tenth century BC or in the twenty-first century AD, proudly boasts that it is secular, with practices which are devised wholly from the mind of man, many will think little of God as a Lawmaker and Judge. Then human life may be taken for any imagined reason. Nevertheless, the Almighty has said, 'And for your lifeblood I will require a reckoning ... for God made man in his own image' (*Gen.* 9:5–6).

2. Lamentation

David led his community in expressing grief for the national calamity of widespread death among Israel's courageous defenders. Especially did they express sorrow and a sense of loss for the shedding of the blood of the royal family. Those who have the hope of eternal life do not deny the heartache nor avoid the tears and disquiet of spirit in the hour of death for those whom we love. When friends and loved ones depart, we are afflicted.

In the contemporary scene, there has come into some circles a silly notion that the death of saints should be celebrated as a triumph. This is simply not a biblical view. It is true that we do not sorrow as those who are without hope.

But we do sorrow. Death is the wages of sin (*Rom.* 6:23). Death is, therefore, not a natural passage to better things. It is the curse of the law, and its consequences will not be reversed until the day of resurrection. The people of God do raise their hearts and voices in lamentation. Jesus knew that, in but a few moments, he would raise Lazarus from the dead, yet our Saviour still wept at the tragedy (*John*

11:35). It is inappropriate to make funerals the occasions of laughter.

3. A Titbit for Bibliophiles

It was the habit in ancient times to compose odes to mark great moments in the military histories of nations. Israel entered into this practice frequently. On this occasion of his nation's defeat on Gilboa, David composed a eulogy to Saul and Jonathan. The inspired writer mentions in 2 Samuel 1:18 that he had copied the eulogy from the *Book of Jashar* (or *Jasher*).

The writer of Joshua also copied verse from the Book of Jashar (*Josh.* 10:12–13), in this case concerning the Valley of Aijalon.

Still earlier Moses had copied from *The Book of the Wars of the Lord* (*Num.* 21:14–15) and from *The Book of the Generations of Adam* (*Gen.* 5:1). Perhaps the last was written by Noah or was carried by him on the ark from the antediluvian world. Many such books, now lost to our modern world, are cited by Scripture as sources used by inspired writers.

4. Eulogy

David's poetic eulogy has three verses (not of equal length). Each begins with the same wail, 'How the mighty have fallen!' (*2 Sam.* 1:19, 25, 27). Throughout the eulogy, the eye of his imagination surveys the heartbreaking scenes of battle, like so many he had personally observed.

In the first verse David grieves as a patriot. The beauty (or glory) of Israel has been slain on her mountains in this defeat (*2 Sam.* 1:19). With a sense of modesty and shame he wishes the news suppressed. It should not be told in Gath or Ashkelon, cities of Philistia, where young women would dance and sing that so many of Israel's soldiers had been slain (*2 Sam.* 1:20). Even Mount Gilboa (personified) should withhold dew, rain, and fruit in sorrow (*2 Sam.* 1:21). David's mind fixes upon a discarded shield on Gilboa. It is tragically rusting, not oiled with care (*2 Sam.* 1:21).

But then his attention turns to the king and his son Jonathan. These were effective, mighty, courageous warriors! They loved one another and remained united in death! Swifter than eagles! Stronger than lions! (*2 Sam.* 1:22–23). Finally David cries to the women of Israel, formerly enriched by the spoils of war from the swords of Saul and Jonathan: they must weep at the loss of their patrons! (*2 Sam.* 1:24).

In the second verse of his eulogy David grieves as a friend. Saul has been treated generously in his death by David. There is not a word about sin, abuse, and oppression. Yet his heart is full of sorrow for Jonathan. David is distressed at the loss of his brother! All his memories of Jonathan are exceedingly pleasant. He extols the love and loyalty of a man whose heart was one with his own.

The third verse of the eulogy is a concluding moan which quickly trails off. 'How the mighty have fallen, and the weapons of war perished!'—scattered across Gilboa and broken.

Interestingly, much of the poetry of the Old Testament is the composition of mighty warriors. David has forever inscribed tributes to Saul and to Jonathan. Jonathan we understand, but Saul?

There is a command in the New Testament which is hard to fulfil, yet David's eulogy embodies it well: 'Love your enemies, do good to those who hate you, bless those who curse you, pray for those who abuse you' (*Luke* 6:27-28; see also *Matt.* 5:44). Despite years of persecution by Saul, there is not a bitter word from Jesse's son. This is not native to the human heart. It is rather a fair flower planted by God's grace.

When our Lord wept at the tomb of Lazarus, biblically-taught Jews observed, 'See how he loved him!' (*John* 11:36). Death is for all who experience it a moment of dishonour, shame (as one suffers the curse for sin), and weakness (as one falls to the hideous enemy, death; *1 Cor.* 15:43). When any we love suffer death, right-thinking men will mourn.

17

CIVIL WAR

2 Samuel 2:1–3:1

David was about thirty years of age when Saul and Jonathan fell in combat against the Philistines on Mount Gilboa. He already had extensive military experience and success. He also possessed an intimate knowledge of the day-by-day operations of government. Behind him now was a dashing life of adventure and intrigue. No great kingdom had been subdued by David. No great riches were amassed. He sat amidst the rubble of Ziklag. Yet deep lines of character had been carved by God's providence within this young man's spirit. As in days gone by the Lord had prepared Joseph in slavery and Daniel in exile, so now he moulded the spirit of him from whose line the throne would never pass.

1. Seeking Guidance

Should David return to Judah? If so, to what city? The warlord asked for God's direction of his paths. He was told to go up to Judah, to the region of Hebron. His small army and their households followed the directions of divine revelation. During exile in Ziklag, David and his troops had regularly sent spoils of war to the elders of Judah. In response the men of Judah now anointed David as their king (king of one of the twelve tribes of Israel). How seldom was all of Israel united under one king! Do we marvel that all true Christians do not reflect their oneness in Christ?

David's first act as King of Judah was to send emissaries to the leaders of Jabesh Gilead. These had been the first Jews defended by King Saul, in their case from the oppression of Nahash the Ammonite (*1 Sam.* 11). Remembering the kindness of Saul many years later, the men of Jabesh courageously rescued the bodies of Saul and his sons which were being shamefully abused by the Philistines (*1 Sam.* 31:9–13). They then gave a decent burial to their hero of long ago.

David strongly commended the men of Jabesh Gilead for their grateful and patriotic service to Saul. A generous benediction was sent from Hebron. Further, David announced to these distant loyal subjects of Saul his anointing by the house of Judah. It was a salute of admiration and support from one group of soldiers to another. Implied was the hope that they would in return be friendly to his reign in Judah. A hand of friendship was cautiously extended to bridge the many divisions in Israel which had been created by Saul's impetuous leadership.

The Lord was about to improve the lot of his chosen people. He had been doing so in incremental steps since Moses had led them out of slavery. However, when God arises with fresh blessings in his redemptive work, it is seldom an instantaneous transport to utopian conditions. Raging opposition more often appears to represent Satan's mood and to confuse the scene viewed by the eyes of human judgment. When God sent Moses to Egypt, at first Pharaoh made the plight of the Jews more difficult. When Christ was born in Bethlehem, a slaughter of infants followed. As Messiah taught pure truth and healed multitudes, opposition by scribes, Pharisees, and chief priests became more vocal and more violent.

2. A Rival Appears

David was not yet free to set a tone of peace among the people of God. Jabesh Gilead was on the east of the Jordan River. Another strong man had just settled there. Abner was Saul's first cousin, son of the brother of Saul's father. That made him a cousin to David through the latter's marriage to Michal. Abner had been Saul's chief of staff over his armed forces. Abner had sat beside Saul at the feasts which David had been expected to attend in earlier days. It was Abner who had ushered David into Saul's presence after the youth had killed Goliath. Abner had later joined the search-and-destroy missions that were targeting David.

On the last such mission David had publicly derided Abner for not adequately guarding Saul. If David's rebuke was justified, a permanent enemy was made on that occasion.

When Saul and his three eldest sons died at the hand of the Philistines, Abner led the remaining forces east through Jezreel to the Jordan River and into Gilead, just south of Jabesh. Abner intended to be the new master of Israel. He had a three-fold strategy.

First, he would loosen the grip of Philistine occupation in the region of the Jezreel Plain. It appears that he did so over a five-year period by occasional raids across the Jordan to drive out the victors at Gilboa.

Secondly, he would install Ish-bosheth, a weak fourth son of Saul, as king over Israel (the ten tribes which did not include Judah). The hold of the Philistines was weakened, and Ish-bosheth was crowned in Mahanaim, where Abner would be the power behind the throne.

Third, Abner would menace Judah by marching his forces south-westward toward Judah's territory. This last movement was a direct challenge to the army of David.

David had learned through the years to keep a close watch on forces hostile to him. From his first arrival in Hebron, the cool reception of his message in Jabesh Gilead proceeded to ever-increasing tensions, due to the ambitions and manoeuvres of Abner. It appears that for more than five years David exercised immense self-control. The king of Judah did not provoke confrontations with Abner whose obvious design to rule all of Israel met with seeming success. David would not permit his army to fight even as Abner declared Ish-bosheth king of all but Judah, seemingly dashing the political aspirations of David's own loyal men.

3. War Breaks Out

However, David was the king of Judah! Abner now had military operations underway and was moving to the border of Judah itself. Therefore David did send his men, under the command of Joab, to intercept Abner's troops at Gibeon, just north of the border of Judah. Apparently, even then Joab was under orders not to instigate a battle. The two armies faced each other, separated by a pool, or reservoir.

Abner suggested that twelve mighty warriors from each force enter combat on behalf of their armies (much as Goliath had suggested a contest between himself and one soldier of Israel). Such contests usually erupt into general conflict. In this case all twenty-four contestants killed each other. Then a pitched battle began during which Abner and his troops were forced to retreat as Joab's men overwhelmed them, causing multiple casualties. Notwithstanding the obvious victory of the men of Judah, Joab's youngest brother, Asahel, was personally slain by Abner.

From the time that David fled from Saul into the wilderness, he had been joined by his sister Zeruiah's three sons, Joab, Abishai, and Asahel. All are listed as David's 'mighty warriors' (*1 Chron.* 11). Asahel's outstanding strength was in running. He was 'as swift of foot as a wild gazelle' (*2 Sam.* 2:18). Primitive warfare with sword and spear depended on muscle. We stand amazed as we read the exploits of ancient warriors. Immense (almost unthinkable) expenditure of physical energy by them is impressive.

As the Battle of the Pool of Gibeon spread to all of the two armies met there, Asahel fixed his eye on Abner and began to pursue only him. Even the mighty captain of the host of Israel could not evade or outrun Asahel. Abner looked back at his pursuer and recognized him. He then urged the young man to seek a less difficult battle with a lesser soldier, but Asahel closed the gap between them. In hand-to-hand combat the experienced captain killed David's nephew. This conflict would sow seeds of deep bitterness against Abner in the hearts of Asahel's brothers.

4. Slanderous Accusations

As the battle went against Ish-bosheth's men, Abner re-formed a unit on a hilltop to face Joab once more. Abner's words were wise but revealing of a treacherous heart. 'Shall the sword devour forever? Do you not know that the end will be bitter? How long will it be before you tell your people to turn from the pursuit of their brothers?' (*2 Sam.* 2:26).

Here were profound truths! It is pleasant to no one to observe a ceaseless flow of blood from the sword. Civil war inevitably produces long-lasting bitterness between factions. It is insane for *brothers* to inflict these horrors on each other! What wise advice, worthy to be considered prayerfully before conflict begins within the ranks of God's people, within churches!

Yet we must consider the source of the above statement. Abner was the aggressor. He cared nothing about the sword's devouring, about consequent bitterness, or about slaying brothers, so long as it advanced his personal ambitions. When all was going against him in the fight, he appealed in these terms to those on the side of righteous self-defence. He so stated his argument as to imply wickedly that Joab was at fault for not having considered these outcomes.

5. Gradual Success

Joab, who had lost a blood brother at the hands of this scoundrel, blew the trumpet to call his victorious men away from the slaughter. It appeared that an evil man had escaped a swift destruction. However there was a two-year war between the house of Saul and the house of David (*1 Sam.* 3:1). With each subsequent incident of conflict, David and Joab grew stronger, while Ish-bosheth and Abner became weaker.

Ascending the throne of Israel was no simple procedure. For David long trials intervened between his anointing and his actually reigning. In this he was like our Saviour, whose path to the throne at God's right hand was never uncontested. Christ's was a long war, not with pagan forces, but with scribes, Pharisees, and priests. A cross and a tomb were his, suggesting at the time utter defeat.

Do we think that our lesser goals within the kingdom will be gained without many a sigh, many an enemy from unexpected quarters? Some conflicts cannot be avoided if truth is to prevail in the cause of God's kingdom. May we have the patience of David, and of One greater than David, to withhold patiently the powers at our command. The Lord is able to deliver his servants at his appointed hour.

As observers of the history of David, we grow impatient to see him prosperously ruling over all of Israel. There are so many difficult obstacles for him to overcome; so many long years of frustration before he receives what God had promised would be his. As delays mount in number and serious rivals threaten his life many times over, it becomes clear that a promised kingdom is not entered without much tribulation. His story is our story as well (perhaps on a smaller scale in our case).

The Almighty, as an artist, paints upon a vast canvas of skies, mountains, valleys, streams, and oceans. To him, the Architect of providence, worlds, nations and long eras of time are building blocks. Eternal purposes of grace took millennia to prepare the scene at which the Lord would save his people from their sins. More millennia would be spent to build his church and to make every knee bow to him. Does it surprise us that we are prepared over long decades for our service?

Children want to see outcomes in a day. Many wish their own lives to be compressed into a few moments during which their victory and success will become apparent to all in this world. Then, they hope fondly, most of their adulthood may be spent taking bows and receiving applause.

A more mature view is the perspective of those who wish to see Christ at his second appearing, then to hear from his own lips, 'Well done, good and faithful servant ... Enter into the joy of your master' (*Matt.* 25:21). This is what all of history is preparing for believers. God prepares us to receive it through all of the occurrences of our lives. Then, for most, death and resurrection come before we hear his gracious voice say, 'Well done!' Meanwhile, the servants are to be faithful to their Master.

18

CIVIL WAR STUMBLES TO A CONCLUSION

2 Samuel 3

Scripture weaves the drama of history in a more breathtaking style than does the fiction writer. Israel's king had died on Mount Gilboa as a result of a Philistine invasion. For more than seven years the nation was then divided into two power factions. David was king in Judah at Hebron; Ish-bosheth, son of Saul, was king in Mahanaim, having the allegiance of ten tribes in Israel. David was the chief figure of his little kingdom. However, Ish-bosheth was very weak, and was being propped up by his father's military commander, Abner.

During the last two years of this division of the nation there were constant skirmishes between the forces of the two kings. These had been provoked by Abner's aggressive threats at the Pool of Gibeon. None of the countless incidents of conflict was decisive. Yet, as the hostilities were grinding on, David's strength increased and Ish-bosheth's diminished. Although Abner was not militarily effective against David, he was significantly consolidating his supremacy over Ish-bosheth.

1. Cultural Circumstances

2 Samuel 3 begins by describing David's growing harem. There were six wives who had borne him six sons. This harem would grow yet larger, and a part of its growth would arise from the process of uniting the nation under him. This aspect of Old Testament behaviour, permitted 'because of your hardness of heart . . . [though] from the beginning it was not so' (*Matt.* 19:8), was an ugly feature of David's domestic life. It would create family squabbles too full of intrigue for a wise ruler of national and international affairs to manage successfully. In addition, it would bring David to the brink of ruin and to long-lasting sorrows.

The scene then shifts from Hebron to Mahanaim, to Ish-bosheth's household. When kings had harems, they were inherited by the new rulers along with the thrones. Thus a faithful son of Saul would care for Saul's wives and concubines, but a rival who captured the kingdom would use them as his own. From the harem of Saul, now under Ish-bosheth's care, Abner took one of the concubines to himself. It was a new level of impertinent contempt for Ish-bosheth. Everyone knew that he who took a king's wife intended to have his throne as well.

This event brought immediate crisis to the capital of the ten tribes of Israel. Ish-bosheth rightly confronted Abner for his misdeed. However, the king had neither personal nor political power to oppose the mighty Abner.

At the mild rebuke of Ish-bosheth, Abner flew into a rage. He let the king know that he owed it to Abner alone that he had not been delivered over into the hand of David. As a result he swore that he would personally make David king from Dan to Beersheba. Perhaps Abner had already realized that David's star was rising and that a personally advantageous way must be found to change sides. He would use this quarrel with Ish-bosheth as the launching pad for gaining influence in David's kingdom.

2. Rapprochement

Abner made good the oath which he had made in his angry tirade. Without apology for past opposition to David, and arrogantly presenting himself as an equal to the king in Hebron, Abner asked for a covenant with David in exchange for his delivering the ten tribes to David's rule.

David responded positively to Abner's emissaries with but one provision. He insisted that Abner would never see his face unless he first returned to him Michal, daughter of Saul, who had been David's wife, but who later had been given by her father to another.

This deal having been arranged behind Ish-bosheth's back, David sent messengers to Saul's son demanding the return of Michal. With his king's consent Abner brought about the delivery of David's first wife to him. Abner also hastened to speak with all the elders of Israel. He made two salient arguments to them: First, for a long time they had really desired to have David as their king. Secondly, the Lord had promised to save Israel from her enemies through the hand of David! 'Now then bring it about', he urged (*2 Sam.* 3:18). Abner made special efforts to prepare the tribe of Benjamin for the exchange of power. After all, Saul had been a Benjamite.

Abner then took twenty men with him to hold discussions with David. The king of Judah had prepared a special meal of welcome for them. In discussions over the meal Abner disclosed to David that all was in readiness. He would leave at once to assemble all Israel for a coronation of David. The civil war would be over. David would be king of all. Obviously Abner would have an important position in David's administration. There was peace between David and Abner. They had arrived at a covenant.

3. Intervention

Entering David's court at just that moment was Joab! He was still in battle gear, leading the triumphant van of spoil from a battlefield. Those Joab met upon his arrival began to give him the latest news. Abner has consulted with David, they tell him. They have made peace. David has sent him away with his blessing on some mission. All of this was completely new to David's second-in-command. The king had not even advised Joab. Nor had the monarch thought to ask Abner for an apology for the slaying of Joab's brother Asahel. David had wanted the removal of an insult to himself (losing his wife Michal), but he had never considered what offences by Abner to others in his family might create havoc within his inner circle.

Joab burst in upon the king with concerned rebuke and with arguments that Abner was a scoundrel dangerous to David's well-being. No doubt Joab's judgment of Abner's character was sound.

Saul's former military chief was a man of selfish ambition. His were actions of immorality and of brazen insult to his former master Ish-bosheth. Abner was a man of treachery, even now plotting the downfall of the household of Saul to which he was related and to which he owed his prominence. These well-established vices had in the past been employed against David. He was not a man to be trusted at this critical moment when David sought to consolidate power in the nation.

Of course Joab and Abishai carried revenge in their hearts because Abner had killed their brother in combat. Joab was not beneath acting as an independent strong man. He seemed usually to act in loyalty to what he thought was David's interest. In this instance it may be that he delivered David from much intrigue and from spending many difficult hours trying to manage a character like Abner.

Yet Joab, in his fury, did not wait to learn of the covenant between David and Abner. At the moment Abner was being fully faithful to his agreement with David. The king was not naïve. He may well have considered how he would keep an eye on his new ally, a man filled with proud and selfish ambition linked with disloyalty. Joab left the king as abruptly as he had interrupted him. To his mind, there was no time to waste on hearing David's reasoning. Immediate action was essential.

Messengers were sent by Joab to recall Abner for further consultation. This he did without David's knowledge. As Abner arrived back at David's seat of power, Joab assassinated the strong man of the north. Thus was the coronation of David aborted once more. And thus was favour for David among the ten tribes and their elders called into serious question. What was David to do?

Strong and decisive men of action are required for the effective administration of nations, large businesses, and large churches. Ish-bosheth could not have reigned without Abner. David would be weakened without Joab and Abishai. Yet these men do not always act in the true interest of their sovereign. Often personal ambition and carnal interest dominate their motives. David would have been cutting off his own right arm to prosecute Joab for the murder of Abner. Holding high office has its unpleasant moments of being unable to keep one's integrity unsullied by another's criminality. Abner the traitor! Joab the murderer!

Where there is concentrated economic and political power, there will be corruption. We do believe in the depravity of all men. We do believe in temptations of the devil which appeal to lusts for wealth and influence. These realities are drawn to governments as surely as metal is attracted to magnets. Why, then, do we react with such shock when scandals arise? We also believe in the grace of God which makes some men noble, if not perfect. Not all politicians are evil, even in places where iniquity abounds. David's integrity was preserved in the midst of great crimes occurring in high places.

Still, the most powerful man of integrity cannot control all the actions and moral decisions taken by those under his rule. It is unrealistic to hold a magistrate personally responsible for all the actions of lieutenants under him.

4. Damage Limitation

David chose to appeal to the sensible judgment of the populace by distancing himself from the deeds of Joab and Abishai:

i. He ordered these two sons of his sister Zeruiah publicly to mourn the death of Abner. And David himself followed the coffin. He led the weeping at Abner's grave.

ii. He composed a poem to clarify publicly that wicked men had killed Abner unjustly.

iii. He fasted for the rest of the day.

iv. He announced to all his servants that Abner was a prince and a great man. This was to show that, in recent dealings with David, Abner was without fault.

v. He notified his servants that he was in weakness, though king, and that the sons of Zeruiah were too strong for him.

vi. He pronounced a curse on the sons of Zeruiah.

Having the highest office does not always mean that a man has a power over inferiors which is sufficient to bring them to justice. David claimed to be unable to bring appropriate retribution on the murderers. Yet he publicly appealed for and received the approval of his citizens for his innocence in the scandalous affair just concluded.

It was a delicate hour for David and for Joab. The establishment of David's kingdom was delayed.

Jehovah sits as king forever. 'Whatever the LORD pleases, he does, in heaven and on earth, in the seas and all deeps' (*Psa.* 135:6; see also *Psa.* 115:3; *Dan.* 4:35). In accomplishing his will the Almighty employs the good works and evil deeds of his secondary agents. Throughout the history of man God is always bringing his plan to pass.

In the midst of all the shameful deeds of Abner and Joab, God was raising a 'good' man to the throne of Israel. He was establishing an ancestor of Christ upon a throne unlike those of other kingdoms. This throne would endure forever and would be used to save multitudes and nations from their sins. Although our Father is never the author of evil, he directs evil's impact for his ends rather than for those of the sinner or of Satan.

Adultery, carnal ambition, treachery, and murder helped to place David on the throne. Widespread hatred and rage against God and his moral law were employed to sacrifice the Lamb of God who takes away the sin of the world. Violence and injustice are frequently channelled by the Lord to cast down the proud and to establish the meek. In the most dramatic instances of these occasions there is scarcely a noble, effective, earthly ruler in sight. Ah, but behind the scenes is the holy and sovereign One who sits enthroned in the heavens.

'Surely the wrath of man shall praise thee: the remainder of wrath shalt thou restrain' (*Psa.* 76:10, AV).

19

CORONATION

2 Samuel 4:1–5:5

David was now about thirty-seven years of age. When he was a young teenager, God's prophet Samuel had anointed him (*1 Sam.* 16:13). This was God's sign of promise that he would be king over Israel. For nearly twenty-five years David had waited for the fulfilment of that promise. There had been indicators that the Lord would fulfil this pledge: heroic deeds of warfare which drew acclaim from the nation; the partial installation as King of Judah (*2 Sam.* 2:4). Yet, the assurances of God through Samuel had been given long ago, and certainly their realization had long been elusive.

1. Waiting on the Lord

Through this prolonged and difficult interval, David learned to 'wait on the LORD'. *Waiting* became a theme of David's Psalms:

> Wait for the LORD;
> be strong, and let your heart take courage;
> wait for the LORD! (*Psa.* 27:14).

Wait for the LORD and keep his way,
and he will exalt you to inherit the land (*Psa.* 37:34).

I waited patiently for the LORD;
he inclined to me and heard my cry.
He drew me up from the pit of destruction,
out of the miry bog,
and set my feet upon a rock,
  making my steps secure.
He put a new song in my mouth . . .' (*Psa.* 40:1–3).

One of the trials of deliverance long delayed, of blessing long withheld, or of prayers long unanswered, is the matter of time. Our God need be in no hurry about these things, for he is eternal. However, we are creatures of but a few years. Our paths incline toward the grave. The sun of our lives sinks toward the western horizon. Because of this we are tempted to question God's providential delays.

Though we are often surprised by this, it is nonetheless true that waiting requires positive effort, with great energy. Maintaining hope in the Lord and his promises is no small matter as the years roll by. Great discipline is demanded of us in holding ourselves back from taking matters into our own hands with carnal means, especially when other voices are justifying us in taking action:

'Wait for the LORD and keep his way' (*Psa.* 37:34).

Watching and praying expectantly for the Lord to fulfil his word of promise exacts exponentially increased faith, supported by devotional wrestlings, as years slip by. For David, half of his lifetime had then passed without fulfilment! For what answers of prayer do you wait, child of God? Does your heart cry, 'How long?'

2. Divine Acts through History

Abner was assassinated by Joab and Abishai. David quickly and emphatically made public demonstrations that he, the King of Judah, had had nothing to do with this act. As for David, he was waiting for the Lord to arise and act. Ish-bosheth, the titular head of Israel, had been empowered in office by Abner's shrewdness and power. Abner's death took all courage from Ish-bosheth. His rule had now become paralysed. Elders throughout the ten tribes quickly became alarmed at the incompetence of their national government.

As lesser magistrates began to take counsel with each other as to how to manage the crisis, the obstacle to their finding a solution was removed. Saul and Ish-bosheth were of the tribe of Benjamin. Two brothers of the Benjamite tribe were each captains of companies of Ish-bosheth's troops. The two conspired to assassinate Ish-bosheth. They entered the palace under the guise of securing grain for their armies. Then they killed the king in his sleep (a man of their own kin), beheaded him, and fled through the next night to David at Hebron.

Rechab and Baanah (the assassins) obviously had concluded that Ish-bosheth's fall from power was inevitable and imminent. Their conspiratorial minds viewed the moment as one to be seized for personal advancement. Thus they boldly said to David, 'Here is the head of Ish-bosheth, the son of Saul, your enemy, who sought your life. The LORD has avenged my lord the king this day on Saul and on his offspring' (*2 Sam.* 4:8). Privately they were confident that the new king would be indebted to them.

Wicked and lawless minds are incapable of believing that others do not reason as they do themselves. Evil is an imbedded ingredient of their logic. They imagine that if selfish ambition moves them to extreme action, the same motive must be dominant in everyone's hearts. 'Every man has his price.'

When Ish-bosheth's head was presented to David, he denounced their treasonable act and immediately executed the seditionists. He had waited on the Lord and had never participated in treachery to advance himself toward the receiving of God's promises. Yet God was directing these ugly acts of history (which the Lord did not incite in wicked men's hearts, nor did his servant, David) to exalt the son of Jesse to the promised throne of Israel.

3. Day of Coronation

The Book of Chronicles gives an account of the vast numbers which assembled at Hebron for this great historic event of David's enthronement. Princes and elders of every tribe were there. All the military commanders came and brought massive divisions with them. 'All these, men of war, arrayed in battle order, came to Hebron with full intent to make David king over all Israel' (*1 Chron.* 12:38). There was a three-day coronation feast. Food poured into Hebron from all of Israel by means of donkeys, camels, mules and oxen, 'for there was joy in Israel' (*1 Chron.* 12:40).

The Book of Samuel emphasizes the speech of the elders of the ten tribes at the time of David's being crowned. With great wisdom the elders expressed three reasons for all Israel's bowing the knee to David. Two of the reasons are drawn from Deuteronomy 17:15. Somehow many commentators have not seen this significant connection. The elders were consciously appealing to Moses' ancient biblical directives. In Deuteronomy, Moses had expressed two qualifications to be sought in a king when Israel possessed the land.

The leaders noted that they were setting over themselves the one whom the Lord had chosen. Their bowing to David was ultimately a bowing to the Lord himself. They were ratifying the choice of the Almighty! 'And the LORD said to you, "You shall be shepherd of my people Israel, and you shall be prince over Israel"' (*2 Sam.* 5:2). They further stated, 'Behold, we are your bone and flesh' (*2 Sam.* 5:1), because Moses had directed, 'You may indeed set a king over you . . . one from among your brothers you shall set as king over you' (*Deut.* 17:15). Thirdly they argued, 'In times past, when Saul was king over us, it was you who led out and brought in Israel' (*2 Sam.* 5:2). In other words they had clearly observed David's effective and faithful leadership in days gone by. With this speech they anointed David for a third time (after Samuel's anointing, and the anointing by the men of Judah). It had been nearly a thousand years since Jacob had prophesied:

Judah, your brothers shall praise you;
your hand shall be on the neck of your enemies;

> your father's sons shall bow down before you . . .
> The sceptre shall not depart from Judah,
> nor the ruler's staff from between his feet,
> until tribute comes to him;
> and to him shall be the obedience of the peoples
> (*Gen.* 49:8–10).

Now, in David's time, the ancient prophecy began to be fulfilled. It would be nearly another thousand years before Shiloh would come! 'The Lord is not slow to fulfil his promise as some count slowness' (*2 Pet.* 3:9). When 'the fullness of time' comes, God fulfils his every promise (*Gal.* 4:4).

The fabric of leadership in God's kingdom should always be woven from the three kinds of thread mentioned by the elders of Israel at the installation of David to his office. Ministers, elders, and deacons of our churches ought to be closely identified with the people they lead. There can be no effective governance without the mutual sentiment of leader and people that we are one. We are the same people and family. Ours is a unity of outlook, affections and purpose. Such an identity between leaders and people is distinct from a situation in which there is a 'star' who attracts and entertains from high above the common man. David was a shepherd, a worshipper and servant of the God of Israel, and a patriot soldier. Therefore his people could identify with him, not merely fear him.

Evidence of effectiveness of administration and of carrying out assignments with faithfulness and competence must be seen in a man before he is given the highest offices of leadership. How many have made the fatal error of putting a man in high office in order to develop leadership qualities. Confidence in leaders must be built by observation that the hand of the Lord is on them in lesser responsibilities, before they are promoted to greater ones.

We have no prophets like Samuel to anoint leaders as the Lord's choices. Yet, with sincere prayer we can ask the Lord to indicate which men should be placed in office. If he can dispose the casting of lots, he can accomplish his will through our selective processes. We do have lists of character qualifications given to us in God's Word to use as a grid for selecting leaders.

4. The Office of King Requires Your Response

David was chosen by God initially to establish the throne on which Christ would reign forever. In being the biological forefather of his own much greater Lord, David also prefigured the Messiah's office of king. First, he had patiently to subdue his people to himself, then to rule over his people and to defend them against all his and their enemies (see *Westminster Shorter Catechism*, Q. & A. 26). Finally, he must destroy their enemies and establish a kingdom of peace and prosperity.

Because David waited on the Lord, and because he gently gathered his flock under his reign, there was willing submission to his throne, and there was a great plenitude of nationwide rejoicing.

Jesus Christ, the eternal Son of God, was conceived by the Holy Spirit in the womb of the Virgin Mary

(*Westminster Shorter Catechism*, Q. & A. 22). He had to be made like his brethren of the human race in order to rule over us. He had to suffer and be tempted in every way as we have been, yet without sin, to rule over us. He identified by his lifestyle and ministry with the poor, the distressed, the sinners. It is as we believingly read the Gospels that we realize that assuredly we are his 'bone and flesh'. The multitudes heard him gladly and sought him out.

Jesus Christ's effective warfare has proven his readiness to rule and defend us, to defeat our greatest foes, and to lead us into peace with God. He alone faced down the roaring lion, Satan, in the battle with temptation. He mightily cast out demons who held men in bondage throughout his ministry. He became a curse for us, enduring for others the just curses of divine law, and diverting God's wrath from his sheep. He entered into the black cavern of death and conquered that giant, emerging victorious after three days. As the Victor over sin, death, and hell, his reign is commended to us.

The capstone of all of this is that Jesus Christ, though rejected as king by Gentiles and Jews alike, has been made Lord and Christ by Almighty God. This same Jesus is assigned by God to judge living and dead men on the last day of history. Who better to rule over your life and your everlasting future?

He has not come to you with bloody sword or raised spear. Jesus approached with good news for the broken-hearted, for prisoners, and for the oppressed. It was with gentle entreaties and kind invitations that the Son of God sought disciples. He has sent armies of witnesses to his greatness, to plead with you to bow and to kiss the ring of the Lord whom God has placed upon the throne. With gentle reasonings and the Holy Spirit's wooings you are called to join the vast assemblage round his throne, and to bow in homage before him. Make your heartfelt pledge of allegiance to Jesus' reign and his commands. Join the shout of 1 Chronicles 12:18, 'We are yours, O [Christ], and with you, O son of [David]! Peace, peace to you, and peace to your helpers! For your God helps you.'

It is something to acknowledge in your reason that God has received this Jesus, son of David, son of Abraham, and has made him Lord over all. It is more to add the recognition that Jesus has victoriously fought the mightiest battles for his people already. It is yet more to admit that he is one of us, true man, the one chosen by God to be king. But beyond having the information, have you approached his throne at God's right hand (by prayer), bowed your knee in irreversible allegiance to his authority and cause, and told him of your being his devout servant henceforth? Have you entered into the thrilling acclaim of Jesus as Lord over all forever and ever? The chief of sinners have done so, sometimes with trembling. What of you?

There is feasting here! Enter the joy of your Lord!

> Crown Him with many crowns,
> The Lamb upon His throne;
> Hark! how the heavenly anthem drowns
> All music but its own.

Awake, my soul, and sing
Of Him who died for thee,
And hail Him as thy matchless King
Through all eternity.

Matthew Bridges
& Godfrey Thring

20

THE CITY OF DAVID

2 Samuel 5:6–25

It appears that, prior to his coronation, David had given thought to the location of the seat of government for a united Israel. When Saul had been anointed king of Israel he had ruled from his home town of Gibeah. It seems that he held court under a tamarisk tree (*1 Sam.* 22:6). David did not intend to move the seat of government to Bethlehem or to retain it at Hebron of Judah.

1. Zion

A suitable capital for the entire nation must be established. Because David expected the nation to be enduring, the chief city must stand in a defensible position. His eye had been on Mount Zion. It possessed the natural defences of steep valleys on three sides. Atop the mountain was the then small city of Jerusalem. It was there that Melchizedek had lived during Abraham's lifetime.

When the Jews conquered the land of promise under Joshua's leadership, the Jebusites held this region. Shortly after Joshua's death the tribe of Judah attacked the Jebusites at Jerusalem and burnt their city (*Judg.* 1:8). Yet, it seems that a Jebusite enclave had never been dislodged from the citadel built south of the city on a precipice which plunges into the Kidron Valley.

Before sending his newly enlarged army to their homes, David led his troops against the Jebusite fortress. As the king's forces came into lines of battle, he was mocked by the Jebusites. Complacent from a long history of safety in their stronghold, the heathen defenders claimed that their defences were impregnable, even when defended by the blind and the lame. 'You will not come in here', they called out to David (*2 Sam.* 5:6).

As newly-crowned king, David offered the various officers under his military command a competitive challenge. Their task was to see who could best devise a scheme to lead his forces in a penetration of the seemingly invincible defences and to begin the actual slaughter of the Jebusite defenders. The prize held out was that the successful officer would become the chief captain of Israel's host.

David was still angry with Joab for the recent assassination of Abner. His nephew had not kept to his subordinate position in that exploit and had greatly complicated David's rise to power. So now that the enlarged national army must be reorganized, David would not promote the troublesome Joab but rather would seek a new man of valour to lead his warriors. However, Joab reached the heights first and became chief and captain after all (*1 Chron.* 11:6). Because of his promise, David became unhappily linked for life to a chief of military staff whom he did not wholly trust. From that day the stronghold was called 'The City of David'. Fortifications to the north toward Millo were also strengthened.

2. Enemy Invasions

Before David actually moved into his new home or finished fortifications at Jerusalem, the army faced two invasions by the Philistines. As soon as news reached the Philistines of David's coronation over all Israel, they determined to destroy him before he consolidated power. As Israel's arch-enemies positioned themselves in the Valley of Rephaim, David inquired of the Lord: Should he go up against the Philistines? Would the Lord deliver them into his hand? He was directed to attack and was assured of victory.

What a splendid beginning for Israel's king! He sought the word of God for direction. When he had in fact defeated these foes he declared, 'God has broken through my enemies by my hand, like a bursting flood.' His army had indeed overwhelmed the heathen like a rushing torrent of water. As the Philistines fled, they abandoned the idols which they had carried into combat. David ordered that these be burned (*1 Chron.* 14:11–12). Lifeless idols cannot defend their cause, as the living God had done when the Philistines had captured his ark of the covenant (*1 Sam.* 5 and 6).

As soon as the Philistines could regroup they invaded the Valley of Rephaim once more. Again David inquired of the Lord. This time the Lord instructed David not to make a frontal assault. Rather he was told to circle round to the rear of his enemies. Even then his forces were to await 'the sound of marching' in the tops of the balsam trees (or shrubs). This sound would indicate the Lord's preceding his troops in the attack upon the Philistines. Again victory ensued upon obedience to the word of the Lord.

In all our conflicts with enemies within and without, we too must look to the Lord for direction. Recognizing that we have neither strength nor wisdom against the forces arrayed against us, we must expectantly search God's Word (*2 Sam.* 5:19, 23). The Lord *must* go out before us if any of our strategies are to be effective (just as his marching led Israel into battle in *2 Sam.* 5:24). We depend utterly upon his power. We must maintain a spiritual sensitivity to the Lord's presence, advancing quickly and not lingering behind when he bestirs himself. Finally, all glory must be given to the Lord in victories. Our praises must be given unstintingly and with continuing humility. Every battle is the Lord's (as David indicated in *2 Sam.* 5:20).

These three exploits illustrate the fact that 'David became greater and greater, for the LORD, the God of hosts, was with him' (*2 Sam.* 5:10). It was also true that 'the fame of David went out into all lands, and the LORD brought the fear of him upon all nations' (*1 Chron.* 14:17).

3. An Important Ally

Among those who were attracted to David by these conquests was Hiram, the Phoenician king of Tyre.

Tyre and Sidon were the great merchant centres of the Mediterranean world in those days. Dealing in the trade of the best of all commodities, these cities had highly skilled craftsmen to work in woods, metals, gemstones, perfumes, and fabrics. A king like David, just rising to power, would have been a great prospective customer.

Hiram was not disappointed. After forming an alliance with the King of Israel, he provided the materials and workers to build a palace for David in the stronghold of Zion. Years later he was to provide the same services as Solomon built the temple and a number of palaces and storage cities. It was to prove a long-standing and lucrative relationship for Hiram.

As we have seen in former relocations, the account of David's move to Jerusalem includes an account of an expanding harem, both of concubines and wives. Six sons had been born to David at Hebron; thirteen were born at Jerusalem. These numbers do not include his sons by concubines (*1 Chron.* 3:1–9).

4. Amazing Links of History, Heaven, and Eternity

Our New Testament begins with 'Jesus Christ, the son of David, the son of Abraham' (*Matt.* 1:1). Not only do these three historic figures share a genealogy, but also they are each major figures in the purposes of God's grace. They each walked in Jerusalem at important moments of their lives.

Abraham visited the city after he defeated a number of heathen kings in order to release Lot from captivity. In these environs he worshipped with Melchizedek, the priest of the Most High God (*Gen.* 14:17–20). On another occasion, it was near here that he offered up Isaac on an altar, receiving his son back (as if resurrected from the dead) through a substitutionary ram provided by the Almighty (*Gen.* 22).

David also walked here after fierce combat with his enemies. He received in Jerusalem the promise that God would establish his throne forever (*2 Sam.* 7:16). The Sweet Psalmist of Israel composed Psalm 110, in which he foretold the coronation of his descendant, the Messiah, along with his installation as high priest forever after the order of Melchizedek. This priesthood of Jesus was sealed with God's oath.

Late in his life David at Jerusalem provoked the Lord to anger. The angel of the Lord stretched out his hand over Jerusalem to destroy it. The angel was positioned by the threshing floor of Araunah the Jebusite. David purchased that site from Araunah, and there he offered a sacrifice to appease the wrath of the Almighty (*2 Sam.* 24). On that parcel of ground the temple was to be built a few years later.

Thus Jerusalem, through Abraham and Melchizedek, later through David, and still later through Christ, became the scene of some of the most remarkable events of worship and of actual redemption of sinners throughout all history. The moments of worship were profound for the men present at Jerusalem in ancient times. Yet, as we are reminded by the martyr Stephen (*Acts* 7), one need not be in the earthly Jerusalem or in Solomon's temple to approach God in worship.

The writer of Hebrews teaches us that tabernacle and temple in Jerusalem were only the copies and shadows of heavenly realities (*Heb.* 8:5). Our high priest Jesus, the son of David, the son of Abraham, now is 'a minister in the holy places, in the true tent that the Lord set up, not man' (*Heb.* 8:2). He is 'seated at the right hand of the throne of the Majesty in heaven' (*Heb.* 8:1) which is merely shadowed in Jerusalem's temple and palace. Through the blood which Jesus shed in the realm of time at the earthly geographic site of Jerusalem, a way was made for us to enter into the Most Holy Place (in the heavenly Jerusalem, prototype of the earthly temple) as we worship. Ours, then, is the reality of greater nearness to God, and this may be experienced anywhere in this world, as our souls ascend into the presence of the Majesty in the heavenly Jerusalem (*Heb.* 9:8–11; 10:19–22).

Jesus the Messiah entered into mortal combat at the earthly Jerusalem with the principalities and powers of darkness. Here Christ's heel was bruised, even as Christ bruised the Serpent's head. Here Jesus Christ rose from the dead; from here he ascended into heaven, and upon this place he first poured out the fullness of the Holy Spirit upon the church. In earthly Jerusalem, at the first church council ever held, it was declared that Gentiles believing in Jesus Christ and being included with Jews in one church, marked the rebuilding of David's tabernacle which had fallen down (*Acts* 15:15–18; *Amos* 9:11–12).

Jerusalem became the biblical name for the assembly of worshippers in the heavenly throne-room from which the Messiah administers his worldwide kingdom in this age (*Rev.* 4-5). When this age ends there will be a passing away of the first heaven and earth. In its place will be a new heaven and a new earth. Then the holy city, the New Jerusalem, will come down out of heaven from God into the new earth. At that time God will dwell with men (*Rev.* 21).

David ushered 'Zion' and 'Jerusalem' into our frequently-used religious vocabulary. Jerusalem is an effective figure of the blessedness of the saints. Her name means 'possession of peace'. For the earthly city this has long been an elusive reality. Not so for the New Jerusalem, now in the heavens, and for her citizens both in heaven and upon earth. This Jerusalem is a fortress whose walls keep out all who destroy and defile.

Jerusalem is the dwelling place of the King. *His* beauty is her chief attraction. *His* fame draws every resident to him. *His* presence makes Jerusalem the glory of the universe. Of course we speak of the reigning Jesus, great David's greater Son. David himself will worship in this Jerusalem: 'The LORD said to my Lord . . .' (*Psa.* 110:1). Abraham will receive his inheritance here. All who have faith in the Son of God will sit down together with Abraham in the joyful kingdom of heaven (*Matt.* 8:11). The feast will be in Jerusalem, when it has come down out of heaven to the earth!

21

BRINGING THE ARK OF GOD TO JERUSALEM

2 Samuel 6

No other king of Israel was so seriously absorbed in the issue of how his people worshipped as was David. He personally composed the core of the biblical Psalter which has served as the foundation of Jewish and Christian musical expression in worship from his day to modern times. Knowing that Solomon would build a temple for the Lord, David assembled workmen and material (*1 Chron.* 22), and he charged all leaders of the nation to assist in the task (*1 Chron.* 22, 28). He reorganized the Levites (*1 Chron.* 23), the divisions of the priesthood (*1 Chron.* 24), the musicians (*1 Chron.* 25), and the gatekeepers and treasurers (*1 Chron.* 26).

1. God's Ark: Its Symbolism and History

David's very first effort to establish national worship in Jerusalem occurred soon after he moved into his city of David. The monarch rightly recognized the prominent function of the ark of the covenant which had been crafted in the lifetime of Moses. The name of Israel's God was then designated as 'the LORD of hosts, who is enthroned on the cherubim', the angelic figures which overshadowed the ark (*1 Sam.* 4:4). Thus the very presence of Jehovah was with the ark of the covenant.

Within the ark were the Ten Commandments which witnessed against the sins of Israel. Covering the ark was a mercy seat on which was annually sprinkled the blood of the sacrifice on the Day of Atonement. Here was signified the holiness of God and his judgment against all sin. The nation was called to humble itself for its sins and to remember that without the shedding of blood there is no remission. The sacrifices repeatedly pointed to the coming Lamb of God, and the opening of a way into God's presence by the Lamb's blood (*Lev.* 16).

When elderly Eli the priest served at the tabernacle in Shiloh and young Samuel served under him, Eli's wicked sons served as priests also. The sons, Hophni and Phinehas, had superstitiously carried the ark into battle against the Philistines (*1 Sam.* 4), thinking that the presence of this religious relic would insure victory for Israel. Both of Eli's sons died in the Philistine attack; the ark was captured by the heathen and the ark was placed in the temple of Dagon (an idol, part man and part fish) in the city of Ashdod.

God visited plagues on the Philistines, compelling them to send the ark back to Israel. When the ark arrived in Beth-shemesh, some curious Jews looked inside it. Seventy men died for this act of sacrilege! With humiliation the Jews placed the ark in the house of Abinadab in Kiriath-jearim where it was nearly forgotten for fifty years.

2. The First Effort to Transport the Ark

David determined that he would bring the ark out of obscurity! He pitched a tent for the ark in Jerusalem (*1 Chron.* 15:1). Thirty thousand choice men were assembled to attend this precious symbol of God's presence among Israel on its journey. A new cart was provided to transport the ark, and Uzzah and Ahio, sons of Abinadab (who had protected it in its years of obscurity) were given honorary posts. Ahio walked before the cart to lead the way. Uzzah drove the ox cart, holding the ark.

Along the way the oxen stumbled. Uzzah took hold of the ark so that it would not fall from the cart. In anger the Lord struck Uzzah dead! David was very angry in response to God's anger. Their motives had been so sincere! Their worship around the ark had been so emotional and energetic (*2 Sam.* 6:5)!

Now that everyone was afraid of God the project was totally suspended. With confused sulking, David refused to transport the ark to Jerusalem. Instead, he deposited it in the nearby home of a citizen named Obed-edom. His high passions had now plunged into annoyance with and indignation toward God. Oh, what a tragic moment was this!

3. God Regulates His Worship

David had planned and prepared thoroughly for the worship of God on that day. Now one was dead and thirty thousand men were stunned. God was angry with them, and they were angry with God. A beautiful plan had gone seriously wrong. This is a stern lesson for a generation like our own whose people think that they can constantly re-invent worship! It appears that there is never even a question within many as to whether God will be pleased with their own original designs to approach him. All of us need to take note that noble intentions, creativity, and sincerity are not sufficient factors in determining what worship is acceptable to the Lord of hosts, who is enthroned on the cherubim!

God is jealous about the way he is worshipped (*Exod.* 20:4–6, the second of the Ten Commandments). As the *Westminster Confession of Faith* comments on this and other Scriptures:

> The acceptable way of worshipping the true God is instituted by himself, and so limited by his own revealed will, that he may not be worshipped . . . any other way not prescribed in the holy Scripture (XXI:1).

It is the Lord's prerogative to dictate how he may be worshipped. He condescends to allow sinners to approach him, and he carefully stipulates how that may be done. With the recent history of plagues that had fallen upon the Philistines who defiled the ark, and of fifty thousand Israelites who had been slain for ignoring well-known cautions against approaching it, one would have expected that David would have taken more care in preparing to move the ark to Jerusalem.

The Almighty had allowed the ark to return from Philistia into Israel by its being placed on a new cart and pulled along by two milk cows (*1 Sam.* 6). However, this method had been devised by those of worldly mindset, men who were ignorant of God's Word. But *Jews*, unto whom all the prophets and all the Word of God had come, had no excuse for worshipping as do heathen peoples. Acceptable homage to God *must not* arise from the imagination of a worship team, not even one led by David himself! The elements of divine services of worship must arise from the Word of God itself. It is totally unacceptable presumption to imagine that God will receive any inventions of man as ways of approaching him.

Very specific directives had been given to Israel for transporting the ark. The ark was to be covered, not opened to public view. It was to be carried on the shoulders of Kohathites, not on a cart or a wagon. Express warnings had been given that even Kohathites must not touch the ark or they would die (*Num.* 4:5-13). These men were to touch only the poles slipped through rings on the ark.

Of course we do not worship by Old Testament forms today. Roman Catholicism made the mistake of creating its worship from Old Testament precedents, with priesthood, vestments, altars, sacrifices, incense, etc. The ways in which the church is to express worship are stipulated in the New Testament. Many modern practices of Protestants are not to be found among them.

4. A Second Attempt

For three months the ark rested in the house of Obed-edom. During those three months the Lord brought remarkable blessing to that entire household. This was reported to David. During the same three months other information came to David which helped to correct his petulant mood, a state of mind which had been brought about by God's powerful rejection of the king's own elaborate plans to bring the ark to Jerusalem.

New arrangements were now made to renew the journey of the ark. This time the king first called the priests and the Levites saying, 'Consecrate yourselves . . . so that you may bring up the ark of the LORD, the God of Israel, to the place that I have prepared for it. Because you did not carry it the first time, the LORD our God broke out against us, because we did not seek him according to the rule.' So, 'the Levites carried the ark of God on their shoulders with the poles, *as Moses had commanded according to the word of the LORD*' (*1 Chron*. 15:12–15). Instead of giving positions of honour to 'choice men', or men of renown, David looked to those anointed by the Lord.

As on the first attempt numerous sacrifices were offered and multitudes attended the journey with emotional praises. This time the directives of God's Word were given primary attention. Thus the ark arrived safely in Jerusalem. David was thrilled at this advance in national worship. Gifts were given to all who came for the celebratory arrival of the ark. Then David turned toward his home to bless his household.

5. Post-Worship Trials

With his spirits still soaring from ecstatic worship, David was jolted by the sarcasm of his wife Michal before ever he entered the door of his home. How honest are the

Scriptures! The greatest of kings argue with their queens. Men of God who have lofty spiritual flights have troubles at home! Just as pirates attack loaded ships, so Satan brings great temptation to hearts filled with the choicest of spiritual delights.

Michal bitterly objected to David's public displays of devotion. She even despised him in her heart because of them. Royalty simply did not strip itself of dignity. What would the daughters of servants think of his shameless displays? Wearing a common linen ephod, a symbol of servitude, David was praising God. This was not befitting his office in her eyes!

David matched his wife's acrimony. He fired back:

> It was before the LORD, who chose *me* above *your* father and above all his house, to appoint *me* as prince over Israel, the people of the LORD . . . I will make myself yet more contemptible than this . . . But by the female servants . . . I shall be held in honour (*2 Sam*. 6:21–22).

It was an explosive exchange. No soft answer to turn away wrath here!

Always lurking in the background for David was a family out of control. As his star rose in the nation, dark shadows were ever present in the recesses of his polygamous house. Many tragedies befell Michal who had once so loved David. This venomous outburst secured for her a childless life. How many days of worship end in careless words and strife! Joy in the assembly of God's people and benefits intended for the family may be strangled by hostilities within that very family. Sharp words have tragic consequences, as we see so vividly illustrated here.

When anyone attends public worship, what is the state of the family from which he goes? Happy is the man or woman with godly spouse and well-ordered children, whose days of heavenly exercises are reinforced by a pious household. How many must assemble with the church as the lonely representatives of their domestic circles! After experiencing unity in the Spirit with the elect, they return within the doors of their dwellings to receive discordant notes, and perhaps hostile comments about the church. If verbal assaults come from those who share the Christian's hearth, they may bring disaster upon those who utter them. Yet it becomes a further grief to the saint who prays longingly for the well-being of those closest to his bosom.

It is difficult to be a stranger and pilgrim even in one's own nest. How we ought to intercede with him who sits upon the heavenly throne on behalf of those within our churches who live in such situations as these!

22

THE HOUSE GOD WOULD BUILD

2 Samuel 7

When he was about forty years of age David's kingdom had been firmly established. Most of the king's enemies had been subdued, although more wars lay in the future for him. However, instead of being pursued like a partridge on the mountains, David now lived in a cedar palace within the defences of Jerusalem. He enjoyed success and affluence to a very high degree.

1. David's Desire

In triumph as well as in danger David's heart turned toward the Lord his God. Other men of prosperity and high attainment indulge themselves in pleasure and boasting. One thinks of the world-conquering monarch of some years later, Nebuchadnezzar, who mused, 'Is not this great Babylon, which I have built by my mighty power as a royal residence and for the glory of my majesty?' (*Dan.* 4:30).

At this stage in David's life Nathan, God's prophet, had become a confidant and advisor to the King of Israel. David disclosed his thoughts to Nathan: 'See now, I dwell in a house of cedar, but the ark of God dwells in a tent' (*2 Sam.* 7:2). The king seemed to be embarrassed by the contrast. The place of God's worship was quite humble while David's home was luxurious. His instinct was that Jehovah should be shown much greater honour than his servant David. There was an impulse to give the best to the Lord of hosts.

It seemed very obvious to David that wealth must not be all for his own personal consumption. As it had been God who prospered him, so David believed he must return more to the Lord. Surely the Lord had found for himself a man after his own heart (*1 Sam.* 13:14).

Nathan recognized in David's concern an extraordinary spirit not often discovered in the courts of kings. With approval of the love for his God in the king's heart, the prophet hastily encouraged this generosity. 'Go, do all that is in your heart, for the LORD is with you' (*2 Sam.* 7:3). There is an excellent principle to be learned at this point. If prosperity ever turns your mind to spending for the kingdom of God, then it will not be a snare to you.

2. God's Design

Nathan became a spiritual giant in the reign of David. In the end he wrote the history of David's rule. Although his work does not survive, it was used as a reference in the writing of the books of Samuel and Chronicles. At the outset, however, Nathan must learn that right spiritual motive is not sufficient to launch a major change in the worship of God. Nor was the approval of a godly prophet's spiritual impulses sufficient to enable David to build a house for the Lord.

In the night God came to Nathan and spoke to him. 'Go and tell my servant David, "Thus says the LORD . . ."' (*2 Sam.* 7:5). Perhaps the prophet obeyed somewhat sheepishly; for God's word countermanded the warmly felt leadings of both David's and Nathan's hearts. Do we not all need frequently to relearn the lesson from the ill-fated first attempt to bring the ark to Jerusalem? We must inquire of God's expressed will in his Word.

Through Nathan the Lord gently questioned David. For hundreds of years there had been no historic precedent for building God a house instead of a tent for worship. Through those centuries there were ordained priests and prophets chosen by God. None of them had ever spoken of building a house of cedar (*2 Sam.* 7:6–7). Where, then, did David find his scheme?

As centuries of Christendom roll by many true hearts long to see Christ's kingdom on earth prosper more extensively. Men grow dissatisfied with the measures that are taken to honour the Lord. New courses of action are suggested which none of the fathers knew and about which the apostolic Scriptures are silent.

Thus men seek to implement more than the preaching of the Word, prayer and fasting, the sacraments, and the singing of God's praises as part of the worship of his holy name. New doctrines are introduced as though no one in two thousand years of time had before discovered them, yet they are thought to be exactly the missing ingredients needed for our day. However, complete novelty ought to be suspect.

3. The Glory of the House which God Builds

Having made it plain that David would not build a house for God, the Lord, by the mouth of his prophet Nathan, declared that 'the LORD will make you a house' (*2 Sam.* 7:11). It is not what David will build for God but what God will construct for David that will be glorious in the earth! Divine workmanship, not human, will most exalt the Lord and most bless his people. The splendour of God's majesty is supremely honoured by the scheme of sovereign grace. 'For from him and through him and to him are all things', is the leading theme of God's world (*Rom.* 11:36).

Then God unfolded to David his plan for the ages in predictive prophecy. David's personal history is amazingly woven into God's eternal purposes. This house which God will make for David is linked to David's 'offspring' or 'seed'. 'I will raise up your offspring after you, who shall come from your body, and I will establish his kingdom' (*2 Sam.* 7:12). As in God's promise of the offspring of the woman (*Gen.* 3:15), and as in God's promises of Abraham's offspring (*Gen.* 12:7; 13:15; and 24:7), so in God's promise of the offspring of David, the offspring must be taken primarily as singular (*Gal.* 3:16). This offspring is obviously the Messiah.

Nathan's words about the offspring of David have reference beyond any merely human descendant who ever sat on a throne in Jerusalem. 'I will establish the throne of his kingdom forever' (*2 Sam.* 7:13). 'I will be to him a father, and he shall be to me a son' (*2 Sam.* 7:14).

These last words are by divine revelation applied to Jesus Christ, the Son of God (*Heb.* 1:5). 'And your house and your kingdom shall be made sure forever before me. Your throne shall be established forever' (*2 Sam.* 7:16).

However, as in the case of the offspring of the woman, and the offspring of Abraham, so the term 'the offspring of David' also has a plural import. As Galatians 3:26–29 puts it, 'For in Christ Jesus you are all sons of God, through faith. For as many of you as were baptized into Christ have put on Christ. There is neither Jew nor Greek, there is neither slave nor free, there is neither male nor female, for you are all one in Christ Jesus. And if you are Christ's, then you are Abraham's offspring, heirs according to promise.'

In the same way, with regard to promises of an everlasting kingdom and an everlasting throne, these too are ours in Christ. We are 'blessed . . . in Christ with every spiritual blessing in the heavenly places' (*Eph.* 1:3). 'If we endure, we will also reign with him' (*2 Tim.* 2:12). 'The one who conquers, I will grant him to sit with me on my throne, as I also conquered and sat down with my Father on his throne' (*Rev.* 3:21).

4. Temporal Predictions

Mixed into Nathan's prophecy also are references to future occurrences which cannot apply to the Messiah. 'When your days are fulfilled and you lie down with your fathers, I will raise up your offspring . . . He shall build a house for my name' (*2 Sam.* 7:12–13). This is an obvious prediction of Solomon's building the temple which David had desired to build.

Further the Spirit states: 'When he commits iniquity, I will discipline him with the rod of men, with the stripes of the sons of men, but my steadfast love will not depart from him, as I took it from Saul, whom I put away from before you' (*2 Sam.* 7:14–15). These words cannot apply to our Lord Jesus but only to Solomon, and to other sinful kings.

5. The Messianic in David's Own Writings

Apparently David meditated on the promise of an everlasting kingdom with an everlasting throne. According to Peter and his sermon on the day of Pentecost, David understood that it was the Messiah who would reign forever on this throne. Being himself a prophet, as the Spirit carried him along in writing the Book of Psalms, he expanded the understanding we have of the Messiah's reign. Peter quoted two texts out of David's Psalms to establish the fact that David understood that Christ was the fulfilment of this promise through Nathan.

First, Peter quoted Psalm 16:8–11. Then the apostle commented on the passage with these words, 'Being therefore a prophet, and knowing that God had sworn with an oath to him that he would set one of his descendants on his throne, he foresaw and spoke about the resurrection of the Christ' (*Acts* 2:30–31). David seemed to conceive of his offspring's coronation as majestic beyond measure. It would occur with Jehovah inviting the risen Christ, possessing the power of an endless life, to sit at the right hand of the Almighty, sharing his heavenly throne.

Secondly, Peter quoted Psalm 110:1. Peter's comment on these words of David was, 'Let all the house of Israel therefore know for certain that God has made him both Lord and Christ, this Jesus whom you crucified' (*Acts* 2:36). Peter did not point to a yet future enthronement of Christ. He declared that Jesus was even then reigning as Lord, in fulfilment of these promises to David.

Shortly afterwards, in the Jerusalem council, James declared his understanding of Amos 9:10–11. In Acts 15:13–18 James stated that the collapsed tent of David had been rebuilt in their day by the work of our Lord Jesus Christ. The evidences of that fulfilment were present as the council met. David's Son and David's Lord, Jesus Christ, has gloriously brought to pass all that was promised to David. In that same Jesus is all of our hope and trust!

6. Eavesdropping on Secret Prayer

Although God had denied David's desire to build a glorious temple as a tribute to the God of Israel, the king could not be disheartened. Such splendid and delightful promises were given in the process of turning down the monarch's request! Such elegant honour was bestowed on David! Nathan's rehearsing of God's word moved King David to go in and sit before the Lord (*2 Sam.* 7:18).

In a secret place the ruler poured out his heart in prayer. This heart-to-heart discussion with the Lord bore the marks of so many of his Psalms.

David was overcome with a sense of unworthiness. He began, 'Who am I, O Lord God, and what is my house, that you have brought me thus far?' (*2 Sam.* 7:18). Repeatedly he presented himself as 'your servant'.

Contemplation of the exquisite privileges of the Messiah arising from his family and thus making his throne eternal compelled him to praise. 'Therefore you are great, O Lord God. For there is none like you, and there is no God besides you, according to all that we have heard with our ears . . . And your name will be magnified forever' (*2 Sam.* 7:22, 26).

David pleaded that God's promises to him would come to pass. 'And now . . . confirm forever the word that you have spoken . . . and do as you have spoken . . . may it please you to bless the house of your servant, so that it may continue forever . . . For you, O Lord God, have spoken, and with your blessing shall the house of your servant be blessed forever' (*2 Sam.* 7:25–26, 29).

Thus should we learn to pray: humbled by God's goodness to us, filled with the praises of a thankful people, and pleading for the promises of God's Word to be fulfilled toward us.

As has been said, 'Prayer is asking God for things which he has promised to give.'

23

REMEMBERING OLD FRIENDS AND COVENANTS

2 Samuel 9

When David became king of all Israel there were battles to be fought to pacify his own land and to establish Israel's defences. When this task was accomplished, David's heart turned to providing a place of honour for the Lord in the land and to erecting a central place for Jehovah's worship in the midst of the nation. Therefore the ark was brought to Jerusalem, and the priesthood was reorganized. However, as we have seen, the Almighty sent a prophet to tell David that he was refused the privilege of building a temple.

At least one reason that it was not time for David to launch a major building project was the necessity of his engaging his energies in foreign wars. The Israelites were surrounded by powerful enemies who had a special hatred of their nation. David, like the Messiah after him, must destroy all of his and his people's enemies. 2 Samuel 8 tells us of victorious wars against the Philistines, against Moab, against Zobah, against Syria, against Amalek, and against Edom.

All of these successful conquests are explained in this way: 'The LORD gave victory to David wherever he went' (*2 Sam*. 8:6, 14). Again we discover that the history of David is *not* about what David did for God, but about what God did for David! David would *not* build a house for God; God *would* build a house for David.

David would *not* bring military victories to the feet of the Lawgiver, as man's gift to the Most High. God *would* preserve David amidst all dangers. The grace of God for man is too often turned into the idea that it is man who does heroic feats for God.

Our humanistic dream is that we may do great things for God. We shall give our genius, our talents, and our strength to him. We will build cathedrals for him. We will round up converts for him. Today the emphasis seems to be, we will put on entertaining extravaganzas for him. Yet the theme of grace is what *he* does for *us!* In conflicts between truth and righteousness on the one side, and falsehood and wickedness on the other, the news is to be found elsewhere than in ourselves. *God* gave victories to David.

If *anything* significant occurs in the kingdom of God, there is a vast incongruity in God's preserving and using unlikely, inept, unwise, and powerless creatures who are opposed by principalities and powers both earthly and heavenly. The Almighty is *not* in a tight spot, needing men to come to his rescue. It is we who, in every hour and emergency of life, stand in need of the Lord to uphold and to deliver us. It is tragic when readers of Scripture barely notice the historic record, 'The LORD gave victory to David' (*2 Sam.* 8:6,14), but rather bolster their humanistic theory that 'David surely gave the Lord's cause a boost in his day.'

1. Spiritual Meditations

In the midst of the repeated clash of ancient armies, with all the horrors and bloodshed of the battlefields, David contemplated who it was that made his campaigns successful. He dedicated much of the spoils of war to the God who prospered him (*2 Sam.* 8:11). He also could not forget the loving fellowship of Jonathan (Saul's son) in the days of his youth. David turned over in his mind the great kindnesses of Jonathan to him. He never before, nor since, had such a loyal friend.

In their youth David and Jonathan were often together in Saul's stronghold in Gibeah. When Saul had become fully resolved to murder David, Jonathan had valued the son of Jesse above his own father. He had risked his life to warn David of the imminent danger. His warning effectively ended the inseparable companionship of this pair of noble warriors. Sensing the nearing conclusion of this association of two sons of God, legendary for its mutual affection and devotion, Jonathan had insisted that a covenant be made between them (*1 Sam.* 20:13–17).

Jonathan's prescient awareness of David's rise and of his own fall had led him to insist that David promise: 1. That when David rose to the throne of Israel he would spare

Jonathan's life, and 2. That he should 'not cut off [his] steadfast love from my house forever, when the LORD cuts off every one of the enemies of David from the face of the earth' (*1 Sam.* 20:15).

When the Lord had cut off numerous and powerful enemies of David, the king recalled his vow. He recalled Jonathan's extraordinary kindnesses to him in his days of weakness. Thus, not only a sense of keeping his word, but also a loving gratitude to his old friend, spurred him on to keep his promise. David yearned to be loyal to Jonathan in the days of his success, 'that I may show . . . kindness for Jonathan's sake' (*2 Sam.* 9:1).

2. Searching for an Opportunity to Be Generous

Saul and his three eldest sons had been slain by the Philistines on Mount Gilboa. His only remaining son, Ish-bosheth, had escaped with his life to the east of the Jordan River. There Abner had installed Ish-bosheth as king. When both Abner and Ish-bosheth were assassinated, no other near relative of Saul would venture into the public spotlight. It was common in the Middle East for a newly-crowned ruler to exterminate the males of the former ruler's household. Any prominence of one who survived this carnage would give rise to whispers that he was a rival for the throne. Then ordinary citizens might kill him to gain special favour with the present king.

There was one grandson of Saul, a son of Jonathan himself, who was living quietly in Trans-Jordan near the bastion where Ish-bosheth had ruled. When his grandfather and his father had died in battle, Mephibosheth (meaning 'Destroyer of Baal') was five years old (*2 Sam.* 4:4). He had been in Gath when news of the Philistine victory had reached the nation's capital. Panic had struck the household of Saul. The Philistine victors would surely plunder the king's home, they thought. A nurse had picked up the five-year-old to carry him away from the place of looming danger. In the haste and confusion Mephibosheth had fallen from the nurse's arms. A severe blow to his feet in the fall had left Mephibosheth lame for the remainder of his life.

In his handicapped condition Mephibosheth depended on the kindness of others. He was living in the house of one such person, whose name was Machir. Yet he still had some normal aspects to his life. By the time David contacted him, Mephibosheth had a young son named Mica. All of this was at first unknown to David, even though he was married to Michal, Mephibosheth's aunt.

David was not content to wait until someone from the household of Saul appealed to him for aid. He searched out the relatives of Jonathan, saying, 'Is there not still someone of the house of Saul, that I may show the kindness of God to him?' (*2 Sam.* 9:3). In just the same fashion, the God of grace sought for us so as to heap his mercy on us. Christ sought each sheep in his fold to bring everlasting blessings to him. The king here was imitating the Most High in his compassion and goodness.

Do you show kindness to others as God has showered undeserved blessings on you? Too many say, 'I'm not aware of those who have needs'! But we must search out opportunities to do good. 'A generous man devises generous things' (*Isa.* 32:8, NKJV). There are widows, the infirm, and prisoners in great need of attention in their sufferings. Our modern society, with its demolition of the family structure, leaves multitudes isolated. Surely you can inquire after them. David did it in the names of God and of Jonathan. We must do so in the names of the Father and of Jesus Christ.

3. An Amazing Interview

From a former servant in Saul's household named Ziba David learned of Jonathan's surviving son. The ruler of Israel summoned Mephibosheth to his throne-room. The bearing of the lame son of Jonathan suggests that he had moments of anxiety in approaching the king. Would the monarch look at him as a threat? Mephibosheth 'fell on his face and paid homage' in silence (*2 Sam.* 9:6). David began the conversation, 'Mephibosheth!' 'Behold, I am your servant', Jonathan's son replied. 'Do not fear, for I will show you kindness for the sake of your father Jonathan . . .' (*2 Sam.* 9:6–7). David spoke lovingly to him. Could there be any other than gentle tones in mentioning Jonathan? Thoughtful words flowed, considerate of Mephibosheth's misgivings. These assuring words calmed the servant of David.

Having resolved to show kindness, David had a list of concrete gifts for Mephibosheth. Far more was delivered than kind words. All of the lands once owned by King Saul were given to Jonathan's son. Ziba, the servant who had cared for these lands in the past, would be given as caretaker of this large estate. Finally, Mephibosheth would receive a position of honour in the court of David. In perpetuity Mephibosheth would be fed at the king's table as though he were one of his own sons! Everyone in the kingdom would know that Mephibosheth enjoyed the special favour of David.

4. A Parable of Christ Blessing Sinners

Are not all sinners like Mephibosheth? We are sons of a king named Adam, who was made lord of all creation. We come from royal stock. When Satan led Adam to destruction all of Adam's children died with him. We were broken and maimed by the fall. Yet we live in the kingdom of Adam's successor, Jesus Christ. Though we are his servants we are not too eager to come before him. We are deserving of death, and we are greatly disfigured by the fall. Christ is a mighty Sovereign who has spoiled principalities and powers, making an open show of them on the cross. We tremble to think of standing before his immediate gaze.

Then one day a messenger arrives. 'The Master calls for you', we are told. He has sought us out and sent for us. We did not take the first steps to meet him. Before we even imagined speaking to Christ, he thought about us! But how can we speak to him? What can we say? We deserve to die! We have nothing to offer him! We are afraid of him!

When the Lord begins to speak to us, 'grace is poured upon [his] lips' (*Psa.* 45:2). He is 'gentle and lowly in heart' (*Matt.* 11:29). He speaks of giving us an everlasting inheritance! He invites us to eat with him. He is knocking and inviting. This Jesus now sits upon the throne of David forever! What an amazing wonder it is that he should reach out to us!

5. An Example to Be Followed

William G. Blaikie in his *The Second Book of Samuel* makes a most unusual application of 2 Samuel 9. He notes that David had once received immense kindness from Jonathan. David believed it was incumbent upon him to return kindness to Jonathan's relatives. All that David gave Mephibosheth was not material. Much was spiritual. Then Blaikie asks the Christian world if it does not have deep obligations to the family of Jesus Christ and Moses, David, Isaiah, Jeremiah, Ezekiel, Daniel, Peter, James, and John!

Blaikie says, 'None are more in need of your friendly remembrance at this day than the descendants of these men. It becomes you to ask, "Is there yet any that is left of their house to whom we may show kindness for Jesus' sake?" For God has not finally cast them off, and Jesus has not ceased to care for those who were his brethren according to the flesh. If there were no other motive to induce us to seek the good of the Jews, this consideration should surely prevail. Ill did the world requite its obligation during the long ages when all manner of contumely and injustice was heaped upon the Hebrew race . . . Their treatment by the Gentiles has been so harsh that, even when better feelings prevail, they are slow, like Mephibosheth, to believe that we mean them well.'

24

DAVID'S TRAGIC SIN

2 Samuel 11

There is an aspect of Scripture that is most unpleasant for Christians to read and contemplate. When God by his prophets has recorded the biographies of great men and women of faith, he has ordained that in most cases their most shameful sins should be catalogued. It is painful to meditate on these accounts. We would rather not know the details of their moral derelictions.

In part this is because we come to love our biblical fathers and mothers in the faith. We, like Shem and Japheth, would like to avert our eyes and to cover over the sins of God's people. Yet God will not allow us to do so, if we believe that 'all Scripture is . . . profitable' (*2 Tim.* 3:16).

Also at work within our hearts is the longing to have human heroes to admire and follow. Although the history of the church, as recorded by man alone, repeatedly turns to the adulation and veneration of certain men and women, Holy Scripture is ruthlessly iconoclastic.

1. A Common Thread in the Lives of the Saints

Noah was found drunk and his nakedness exposed after the flood. Abraham lied more than once and put his wife in danger for his personal protection. Moses flew into a sinful rage in public. Peter denied Jesus three times and later endangered the doctrinal integrity of the gospel. David committed adultery and murder, along with a great complexity of 'lesser' sins. There simply are no ideal mentors, leaders, or shining mortals who are unassailable.

Perhaps the Lord intends to disabuse us of a 'star' mentality in Christendom. An over-estimation of leaders will eventually destroy even the realism of knowing who we ourselves are, so long as we have a corrupt nature and walk through a fallen world.

Hope of being some day 'souls made perfect' must not lead us to imagine that we ever will be that in this life, either in our own eyes or in the eyes of others.

David sinned criminally, after serving as the central figure in exploits for God too numerous to list. Noah fell after long and courageous years of service to God. Peter's downfall came after outstanding feats for his Master. Have not some of our own most grievous acts of lawbreaking occurred in our spiritual maturity, after having spent years of devotion to Christ? At least, the aspects of sinning against greater knowledge and against great mercies already received intensify our guilt.

In David and in us these lapses in loving obedience to the Lord Jesus remind us that all kinds of sinful inclinations lurk in the shadows of our hearts still! To the last breath we must all 'Watch and pray that [we] may not enter into temptation' (*Matt.* 26:41). We have not outgrown the need to have the Lord's Prayer as our daily model. 'And lead us not into temptation, but deliver us from evil', must be our urgent request in every season (*Matt.* 6:13).

2. The Hour of Temptation

We are told that David slipped into his sin in moments of relative idleness. 'In the spring of the year, the time when kings go out to battle . . . David remained at Jerusalem. It happened, late one afternoon, when David arose from his couch and was walking on the roof of the king's house . . .' (*2 Sam.* 11:1-2). After so much intense conflict for the Lord, could he not relax?

How can we be safe from the poisoned arrows of the wicked one? Although we may long for a reprieve from labour, and although all men work better with some relaxation, too much leisure may be Satan's playground. Some of the best means of sanctification are not in facing down the tempter, but in pouring ourselves into useful service to God, so that no time or energy is available for the devil's employ.

The tempter wove an elaborate net quickly. David did, after all, carry his physical desires with him. God had provided legitimate satisfaction for all these appetites. But the lust of the flesh, the yearning for forbidden gratification of these cravings, can flare up in an instant and overpower strong men.

The *lust of the flesh* was aroused by the *lust of the eyes,* an aesthetically beautiful object brought into view. Did not God make our cravings and make these pleasing objects to silence the voice of hunger? David knew God's law, the limits placed on excess. But was he not the king? Who would dare to deny him his wishes? Thus was added the *pride of life*, and the explosive concoction was completed in his heart (see *1 John* 2:15–16, AV). 'And David sent and inquired about the woman' (*2 Sam.* 11:3). He had power and servants to execute his will.

How we need the grace of God to the very end! How we need to abide in Christ every moment! How we need the Holy Spirit for every step of our pilgrimages! So, too, do the godliest among us.

3. The Season of Sin

Holy men of old knew that they should not look on a woman with lust. 'I have made a covenant with my eyes; how then could I gaze at a virgin?' (*Job* 31:1). Holy women knew that they should not present themselves uncovered to public view. David and Bathsheba should each have objected more vigorously to the arranged tryst that followed. Neither should have hypocritically discussed purification laws, as if keeping them made their sin less damning.

It is not only the young man who 'at once . . . follows her, as an ox goes to the slaughter, or as a stag is caught fast till an arrow pierces its liver' (*Prov.* 7:22–23). Women also rush to their ruin in their attempts to attract the attention of men.

Later a hasty message came to the palace. 'I am pregnant' (*2 Sam.* 11:5). Had there been anxious days of hoping that nothing more would come of this sin? But God had caused her to conceive. Now there was a complex maze of problems. How to cover up the whole affair to minimize the damage became a preoccupation for the partners in sin.

Cover-up is the first instinct of a sinner whose evil deeds are about to become public:

> Whoever conceals his transgressions will not prosper, but he who confesses and forsakes them will obtain mercy (*Prov.* 28:13).

Elaborate subterfuge was David's chosen refuge. The Psalms reveal how often in danger he had fled to the shadow of God's wings for help. At this time David was his own enemy. The aid of an offended Jehovah would be of no help. Thus he relied on cunning and deception.

As commander-in-chief, the king summoned Bathsheba's husband Uriah from the siege of Rabbah (the capital of Ammon). How often the modern argument enters a sinner's mind. 'The attraction between us is love. What we do is no one else's business. This is our private affair.' So Satan had dimmed David's awareness that Bathsheba was Uriah's wife and Eliam's daughter (*2 Sam.* 11:3). What the two did in secret profoundly impacted father and husband.

4. Compounding Sin

Uriah the Hittite was one of David's most faithful and mighty of warriors (*1 Chron.* 11:41; *2 Sam.* 23:39). He was well known to the king from his earlier days of adversity and splendid exploits. Now David had stolen the wife of a man of outstanding courage and of special loyalty to him. When the officer arrived at the court in Jerusalem in response to a summons from his king, David feigned a desire for a special battlefield report. Then he sent Uriah home, expecting him to sleep with Bathsheba.

In devotion to his fellow-soldiers who were risking their lives at that very moment, Uriah refused to enjoy the comforts of home. While the military mission continued he would endure hardship with his comrades in arms. He slept at the door of David's palace awaiting further orders.

On the next day David plied Uriah with alcohol and made him drunk. Still the soldier would not go to his house. David's ploy to make it appear that Bathsheba's child belonged to her husband had failed. At this point David's machinations to conceal the truth led him into dark shadows of desperation.

The king determined to enlist Joab in his conspiracy. Joab was the man whom David had publicly rebuked for an act of murderous revenge. David had been so repelled by Joab's lack of character that he had sought to be rid of his services as chief of staff over his armed forces. However, Joab's dark side was just what David now desired. One who was an object of David's dislike thus became his ally, chosen because of his treachery!

Uriah, who was to be the innocent victim, carried a message to Joab requiring him as chief commander on the field to arrange for Uriah's death. David's motive in plotting Uriah's murder was more vile than Joab's avenging of his brother's death had been. The deed was done! David was informed. He feigned lack of concern about the death of Uriah. Bathsheba feigned sorrow for her husband. Then Bathsheba was added to David's harem.

5. An Observer's Response

Had not David written, 'O LORD, you have searched me and known me! You know when I sit down and when I rise up; you discern my thoughts from afar' (*Psa.* 139:1–2)? A later son of David and Bathsheba would write, 'The eyes of the LORD are in every place, keeping watch on the evil and the good' (*Prov.* 15:3). It is futile to attempt to hide sin from the omniscient Lord. 'And no creature is hidden from his sight, but all are naked and exposed to the eyes of him to whom we must give account' (*Heb.* 4:13).

David never forgot these things. Yet, to arrange his sin with Bathsheba he had intentionally silenced the fear of God in his heart. Now, panic at the threat of being found out was fuelled by the fear of man. All the lies, the abuse of Uriah, and the murder, were meant to mislead mere mortals. It seemed to David as though his scheme was working. But the palace servants and advisers knew. Joab knew. However, it was now obvious to all that the king would fully employ his autocratic powers to silence any wagging tongue which dared to speak of this matter. Just observe what he had done to Uriah! Still, *God* was watching, the One over whom David had no power.

Between David's cover-up and a not-very-distant confrontation with God's prophet Nathan stands an understated but ominous comment. 'But the thing that David had done displeased the LORD' (*2 Sam.* 11:27).

Patterns of Davidic deceit are not difficult to learn. They are instinctive to sinners' hearts. Mature saints realize that they must quench the fires of the fear of God within in order to satisfy base fleshly desires. First we deceive ourselves that God will not be so angry if we break his law. The voice of conscience is drugged.

When there is danger of our sins being discovered by men, many devices are employed to save us from embarrassment. All the while we continue to refuse to acknowledge the obvious. The chief assault of every sin is against the Lord and his Messiah (*Psa.* 2:2). Attempts to hide from him as did Adam and Eve are the depth of folly (*Gen.* 3:8).

In the end, the sinful things you have done displease the Lord! They have never escaped his attention, interest, or evaluation. His displeasure has consequences. He is a God of justice and truth. He will not be complicit in your misrepresentations of your sins. You will confess and forsake your sins, or you can never prosper again. But there is mercy with God to all who humbly repent at the foot of Jesus' cross.

'Let the wicked forsake his way, and the unrighteous man his thoughts; let him return to the LORD, that he may have compassion on him, and to our God, for he will abundantly pardon' (*Isa.* 55:7). Christ has come not to call the righteous but sinners to repentance (*Luke* 5:32). Take the covers off your sins, and find mercy in Christ. It is to bring you to this that this ugly chapter of David's life is fully told.

25

DAVID'S REPENTANCE

2 Samuel 12:1–14

1. The Lord Seeks David, His Wayward Sheep

'And the LORD sent Nathan to David' (*2 Sam.* 12:1). The Lord of heaven and earth has messages for kings and for all who are in governmental authority. In another era the Most High sent Daniel to a heathen king. 'For there is no authority except from God, and those that exist have been instituted by God' (*Rom.* 13:1). Those who preach God's Word must not be silent in addressing authorities as to the revealed will of God. In Israel prophets usually had special access to the throne-rooms of kings.

David and Nathan had worked closely together in establishing the worship of Jehovah at Jerusalem. Yet it would not be surprising to learn that their relationship had cooled when this command reached Nathan. Almost a year had passed since David had killed Uriah and taken his wife. Bathsheba's child had already been born. Months had gone by during which David later described his spiritual condition thus: 'My bones wasted away through my groaning all day long ... day and night your hand was heavy upon me; my strength was dried up as by the heat of summer' (*Psa.* 32:3–4).

Not only had David committed outrageous sins but he continued for a considerable time refusing to confess, repent, and return to a walk with God. Had we, like Joab, known the full extent of David's crimes, and had we seen his hardened condition of heart continuing over a prolonged period of time, we would have had good reason to question whether he was numbered with the called and elect of God. During this period there was no evidence visible to men that David was any different from Saul, from whom the Lord had withdrawn permanently.

In similar fashion, for some hours in the midnight blackness of Christ's trial and crucifixion it would have appeared to external observers that there was no distinction between Peter and Judas. In any age it is possible for true children of God to appear to our judgment to be like those who finally fall away from the faith.

In the midst of any spiritual declension in men and women which is shocking to us, we must be cautious in our statements. *At the moment* we have *no reason to believe* that these fallen ones, once in our fellowship, are of the called and elect of God. Only God would have known of David's inward experience of sheer misery at his distance from the Lord and of his future repentance. For us, the public repentance of David, Peter, and the scandalous sinner at Corinth (*2 Cor.* 2:6-8) is the only basis of our knowing that the grievous sins of saints are not the same things as those which expose hypocrites.

Nathan was the spiritual man sent by God to restore David, caught in a transgression (*Gal.* 6:1). These are missions which spiritual men do not ever enjoy. The Scripture gives us this outstanding example of the restoration of a sinner 'in a spirit of gentleness'. Rather than speaking with flaming rebuke, the prophet appealed to David's well-instructed conscience and finely-honed sense of justice.

2. A Spiritual Parable

Perhaps the Lord revealed the precise words Nathan was to use. In ancient governments kings were also the supreme judges of the land. Therefore Nathan spoke of a criminal act in David's land which called for his administration of justice. The story is woven round the ever-present conflict between rich and poor, but it also made appeal to David's shepherd's heart. A wealthy man, greedy to keep all the sheep of his large flocks, had stolen the single lamb which a poor man kept as his beloved pet. This much-loved lamb had been killed to provide a 'traveller's' entertainment.

Deeply incensed at the undesignated man's crime, the king issued the appropriate sentence. The rich man will die! David issued his decision with an oath, 'As the LORD lives'! In addition the poor man must receive fourfold for what had been stolen (as Moses had required in *Exod.* 22:1).

The death sentence, however, was David's own invention for a man who would dare to have so little pity on the poor as to commit such a terrible deed.

If we could only stop to consider our own thoughts, we would be amazed to discover that we are all capable of being indignant at the sins of others, while we live with hardened and unrepentant hearts toward our own greater sins! When a well-taught Christian falls into serious sin, he does not lose his keen awareness of righteousness, nor does he lose his high passion for justice, *when other men's sins are in view*.

Wayward Christians in the depths of shameful sins have at times instructed others with great clarity about the law and the gospel to the utter amazement of their depraved companions.

Once David's conscience and sense of justice had been fully aroused, Nathan simply said, '*You are the man!*' (*2 Sam.* 12:7). The rich man in Israel was David himself! The poor man was Uriah. The sheep were their wives, of whom David had many, whereas Uriah had but one, and she so dearly treasured. The traveller was the sexual desire which comes and goes. David would feed his occasional appetite at Uriah's expense. Thus the king had issued a sentence against himself, a citizen of his own realm! He had prescribed death in God's own name!

3. Far Reaching Consequences

As David stood stunned by the sudden revelation that Nathan had been speaking of him, Nathan delivered God's words: 'Thus says the LORD, the God of Israel.' What courage is required of those whom God sends to declare his words, what boldness! But it is possible to combine gentleness with directness and faithfulness to God's announcements, and that is what the prophet had so well done in this instance.

God now rehearsed his numerous kindnesses to David. The Lord had anointed him to be king over Israel. The Lord had delivered David from the murderous plots of Saul. The Lord had given Saul's house and his wives into David's power. The Lord had united Israel and Judah under David's crown. The Lord stood ready to do much more to exalt David. All of these amplified the guilt of David's sin.

Then God's word put David's sin into perspective. The accusation is personal and direct: 'Why have *you despised* the *word of the* L*ORD*, to do what is evil in his sight?' Later, as David prayed over his sin (*Psa*. 51), it was this comment that was embedded in his memory like the barbs of a harpoon. 'Against you, you only, have I sinned and done what is evil in your sight', he sobbed in regretful confession (*Psa*. 51:4). With withering directness God's word said, 'You have struck down Uriah the Hittite with the sword and have taken his wife to be your wife and have killed him with the sword of the Ammonites' (*2 Sam*. 12:9).

Immediately the consequences of these divine chastisements were enumerated.

1. 'Now therefore the sword shall never depart from *your* house because you have *despised me . . .*'

2. 'I will raise up evil against *you* out of *your* own house. And I will take your wives before your eyes and give them to your neighbour, and he shall lie with your wives in the sight of this sun. For *you* did it secretly, but *I* will do this

thing before all Israel and before the sun' (*2 Sam.* 12: 10–12).

Let the alarming phrase ring in the ears of all who labour to cover their sins: 'Be sure your sin will find you out' (*Num.* 32:23). We may sin in the darkness but God will judge in the full light of day. God's litany of punishments for David became the outline of the remainder of his life history.

4. Grace Shines in Humility

At this point in Nathan's rehearsal of God's word, David's inward grace shone brightly. Before God and man David cried in anguish, 'I have sinned against the LORD' (*2 Sam.* 12:13). Although the great monarch had withdrawn from God's fellowship, he was overwhelmed with grief that he had sinned against the One whom his soul loved, whose loving-kindness he had enjoyed through so many years except the last one. The saint is never more himself than in the exercise of a broken and contrite spirit before the Almighty. His confession was directed to Nathan. Perhaps with it there was an imploring tone and look, as if to say, 'What shall I do?'

Again in gentleness Nathan immediately assured him, 'The LORD also has put away your sin' (*2 Sam.* 12:13). Why do Christians who have stumbled cover their sins? Doing so multiplies their grief. 'If we confess our sins, he is faithful and just to forgive us our sins and to cleanse us from all unrighteousness' (*1 John* 1:9), and 'if anyone does sin, we have an advocate with the Father, Jesus Christ the righteous' (*1 John* 2:1). Experience of grace is parallel for those who live under all the administrations of its covenant. How stern God's words to David prior to his confession; how filled with mercy and kindness the instant he repented! 'The LORD also has put away your sin'! Put it away from his accounting books; put it away from his memory against his child. As the New Covenant promise says, 'For I will be merciful toward their iniquities, and I will remember their sins no more' (*Heb.* 8:12). It is put away from David 'as far as the east is from the west' (*Psa.* 103:12). Put away by the Lamb of God, who is our 'advocate with the Father', and 'the propitiation for our sins' (*1 John* 2:1–2).

What a glorious announcement of the gospel! But God's words, 'The LORD also has put away your sin', were held back from application to David until he confessed, 'I have sinned against the LORD.' Because with an oath David had pronounced a death sentence upon himself, Nathan hastened to revoke that sentence upon the authority of God. 'The LORD also has put away your sin; you shall not die' (*2 Sam.* 12:13).

5. God Cannot Deny Himself

It would seem that, in order to confess his sin, David had broken into Nathan's catalogue of temporal judgments which God would visit on the king for his sins. This appears from Nathan's last words in this dramatic visit to the royal court. After assuring the king of God's forgiveness and of God's lifting of the death sentence against him, Nathan continued with one more temporal consequence of David's sin. The child born to David and

Bathsheba would surely die (*2 Sam.* 12:14). 'And the LORD afflicted the child that Uriah's wife bore to David, and he became sick' (*2 Sam.* 12:15). This occurred as Nathan exited from the presence of the king.

Here is a sequence which deserves our meditation. Too many in our day have adopted the liberal theory that the *only* purpose for the punishment of man is remedial. All unpleasant consequences to man for his criminal behaviour, whether those consequences are administered by God or by man, are only for the improvement of the lawless one. This attitude has certainly taken over the minds of church members with regard to church discipline. The only purpose they can even imagine for censures or for withdrawal of church privileges is to win the individual back. The thought is, 'Surely, if a sinner repents, all measures of discipline should be removed.'

Nathan gives us an important reason why God's temporal sanctions against David must be carried through, despite the fact that his repentance had been one of the most thorough and public in the history of God's people. 'Because by this deed you have given great occasion to the enemies of the LORD to blaspheme, the child . . . shall surely die' (*2 Sam.* 12:14, NKJV, NIV). The public honour of God must be upheld!

When the servants of God, and especially those who are publicly used to advance God's kingdom, sin scandalously, the enemies of the Lord attribute their immoral behaviour to the character of the God whom they serve. In public defence of the holiness of God, it *must* be shown that the Lord *and* his church do *not* endorse the sins of his servants. For this reason in particular, Paul instructs Timothy that, if elders persist in sin, they are to be rebuked 'in the presence of all' (*1 Tim*. 5:20).

In David's case, all of the sad consequences in his life flowing from his adultery and murder declare to all the world that the true God is holy and just. All those within God's kingdom *must* learn to fear him.

26

A STUNNING TRANSFORMATION

2 Samuel 12:15–25

It appears that Nathan's visit to the court of David was very brief. The prophet was on a divine mission which he accomplished without dallying. His rapid, crisp comments radically recast the scene and the spirit of David's throne-room. As Nathan told his parable of two men in Jerusalem, the king was poised and self-assured in his responses and decrees. The spine-tingling words of the prophet which followed David's hubris left the ruler as a broken man on his face pleading with God, in the plain sight of his servants.

1. Humiliation and Prayer

Although David's sin was a serious offence to God, and although he had continued long with a hardened and unrepentant spirit, a direct confrontation by God's word elicited a confession and an act of humiliation before God and men. Nathan's prediction that the child born of David and Bathsheba would die (*2 Sam.* 12:14) was almost immediately underscored by a report that the babe was ill (*2 Sam.* 12:15). 'David therefore sought God on behalf of the child. And David fasted and went in and lay all night on the ground' (*2 Sam.* 12:16).

The son of Jesse, so used to praying and praising his God, had long ignored speaking to him about Bathsheba, her son, or his own grievous transgression. Failure to account for our sins before God can cut off the lifeline of prayer.

Suddenly the old springs of prayer in David's heart were reopened. His approach to God was humble, as indicated by David's prostrate position and by his fasting. The earnestness of his pleading with God was also demonstrated by his seven days of continuing in prayer and by his refusing food and other comforts.

2. Faith and Prayer

When, at the end of these exercises in prayer, his servants asked of him an explanation, David answered, 'While the child was still alive, I fasted and wept, for I said, "Who knows whether the LORD will be gracious to me, that the child may live?"' (*2 Sam.* 12:22). As David heard God's word through Nathan, and as he confessed his sins, the embers of faith within his backslidden heart burst into flame, enabling him to pray.

The Lord is a 'gracious' God! Sovereign grace was the foundation of David's prior and present relationship with God. The word here rendered as 'gracious' is translated an equal number of times as 'merciful'.

When we stray into sin and continue in it, our sense of guilt and shame may serve as a dark cloud to hide God's grace and mercy from our view. Thus our faith will be sickly and our prayer silenced or formal, without a sincere approach to God who receives sinners through Christ.

Did not our Lord mourn, 'O faithless generation . . . How long am I to bear with you?' (*Mark* 9:19)? Unbelief weakens prayer and other action. Doubts of God's loving-kindness silence the praying tongue. 'Praying at all times in the Spirit, with all prayer and supplication' (*Eph.* 6:18) is a weapon of our warfare without which we cannot successfully enter spiritual combat. This weapon cannot be put into service without trust in the grace of God.

3. Fasting with Prayer

We need also to take note of David's fasting in connection with prayer. With so much modern emphasis on joy and triumph in the Christian life, large numbers of believers have seldom or never fasted with prayer. Fasting is a refusal to be distracted from what we are requesting of God. It is an expression of wholehearted engagement with God concerning the subject of our petitions from his gracious hand.

David had experienced the grace and mercy of God so often in the past. He *knew* that God's loving-kindness was unfailing to his people. To that aspect of God's character he clung for seven days while his child lived.

Both Old and New Testament point us to *fasting* and prayer. In Mark 9 our Lord Jesus' disciples had failed to cast a demon out of a child. Jesus saved the lad from his dreadful bondage. When his disciples asked, 'Why could we not cast it out?' (*Mark* 9:28), 'He said to them, "This kind can come out by nothing but prayer and fasting"' (*Mark* 9:29, NKJV). There are oppositions from powers of darkness, there are crushing defeats when we fall into sin, and there are family crises, none of which will give way to anything less than prayer and fasting! The gates of heaven must be stormed ardently. Damages by Satan's activity must be undone by diligence and painful effort.

Jesus launched his ministry with extraordinary fasting (*Matt.* 4). The early church launched Gentile missions with fasting (*Acts* 13:3). Paul conducted his ministry with frequent fastings (*2 Cor.* 6:5; 11:27).

Do you at this time experience heavy responsibilities, heavy trials, or heavy guilt for recent sin? Have you fasted and prayed in connection with these difficulties? David did so, in faith, believing in the grace of God. His grace does not remove responsibility from us. Those who trust in God's grace must labour by fasting and prayer. An inability to enter such labour suggests a weak faith in the mercy of God.

In contrast with such weakness of faith, when David and Bathsheba's child died, and David's pleading had been thereby denied, the king 'went into the house of the LORD and worshipped' (*2 Sam.* 12:20). Public worship with the people of God expressed his continuing devotion to God Most High. This was much like Job who went before him, and, having lost his children in tragic circumstances, worshipped, saying, 'The LORD gave, and the LORD has taken away; blessed be the name of the LORD' (*Job* 1:21).

Do you hold public worship of your God to be a vital expression of faith in him?

4. Was God Gracious to the Child?

David had been so insistent that the leaders of his palace must not interrupt his prayer for his son, that when his son actually died they did not dare to tell the king. If he had been so disturbed at the child's illness, they thought, David might lose all sanity at the news of his death (*2 Sam.* 12:18). David guessed the truth from the whisperings of his attendants.

Instead of fulfilling their fears David said, 'Can I bring him back again? I shall go to him, but he will not return to me' (*2 Sam.* 12:23). In this statement is one of David's many expressions of confidence in the existence of human life beyond the grave. He too would one day go to the realm of the dead where his son then dwelt. If this assurance, that he and his son would share a life together in the world to come, is added to the affirmation of Psalm 23:6, 'I shall dwell in the house of the LORD forever', then he may be confessing that his son has preceded him to the house of the Lord.

Elsewhere in the Old Testament there are lessons to the effect that the death of a child is not always tragic for that child, however it may break the hearts of parents. In 1 Kings 14, Abijah, the son of Jeroboam, became sick. The King of Israel sent his wife to the prophet Ahijah at Shiloh to ask what would become of their son. She was told by the elderly prophet that Abijah would die at the time when she arrived back at her home. He was to die *because this child was the only one in Jeroboam's house in whom the Lord found something good.* He was therefore being taken away so that he would not suffer the disaster that God would bring on the rest of Jeroboam's household.

In the case of David and Bathsheba's firstborn also there may have been mercy to the child. Perhaps he was being taken away so that he would not suffer the sword which would never depart from David's house (*2 Sam.* 12:10). This is a principle of God's providence which is often ignored. Isaiah 57:1–2 states, 'The righteous man perishes, and no one lays it to heart; devout men are taken away, while no one understands. For the righteous man is taken away from calamity; he enters into peace.' Length of years is not a blessing if God's wrath is to be widely experienced. Especially does God save the young whom he loves in this way.

5. God's Grace to the Marriage of David and Bathsheba

David's marriage to Bathsheba should never have taken place! Nathan's direct rebuke showed that David's taking Bathsheba from Uriah was an abomination in God's sight. Such actions are clearly forbidden by Scripture.

Sometimes when men sin they begin to hate the object of their forbidden affection. Sinners may begin to despise what once they lusted after, much as Judas hurled the silver pieces at the priests who had purchased the apostle's betrayal of Christ with them. However, ugly as their past acts of sin had been in God's eyes, and vile as was Satan's luring David to depart from God with Bathsheba as his bait, David became a faithful husband to his ill-gotten wife.

'Then David comforted his wife, Bathsheba' (*2 Sam.* 12:24). Wrong as it had been to take her for his wife, she *was* now his wife. The crime was not to be compounded by mistreating her. She too suffered because of the death of their child. David gave attention to her in her grief and comforted her as he could.

Soon Bathsheba conceived and bore to David another son. They called him Solomon, which means 'peaceable', or 'man of peace'. Since David had sincerely repented of his sin and had sought the grace of God earnestly, the Lord was not forever angry with the union of David and Bathsheba. In particular, the Lord loved Solomon, their son. Nathan, who so shortly before had declared God's displeasure with their sin, was sent to pronounce God's choice of name for the child. The Almighty gave him the title 'Jedidiah' ('the beloved of the Lord'; *2 Sam.* 12:25). God keeps his promise, 'For I will be merciful toward their iniquities, and I will remember their sins no more' (*Heb.* 8:12).

How often before had God taken sinners into the direct line by which Messiah would come! The notorious deeds of some of Christ's ancestors from the time before God's grace embraced them have been recorded in Scripture. Let no one who has fallen precipitously into sin imagine that it is now too late for God to receive him, or for God to use him in his kingdom. David's son Solomon too is a direct ancestor of God's Anointed! This Christ Jesus 'came into the world to save sinners', of whom Paul, and David, and Bathsheba are chief (*1 Tim.* 1:15). Our God is able to sanctify the lawless marriage and its fruit.

6. Grace to All Who Repent

There are times when strong rebuke is required to awaken sinners who are asleep with respect to both faith and prayer. Yet the severity of the tone of God's Word and the stinging nature of his chastisements are never intended to suggest that there is no way of returning to the Lord. On all who turn in repentance he will have mercy, and will abundantly pardon.

In 1 Corinthians 6:9–11 Paul addresses the Corinthian church. 'Do you not know that the unrighteous will not inherit the kingdom of God?' What he means by 'unrighteous' is then enumerated: 'the sexually immoral . . . idolaters . . . adulterers . . . men who practice homosexuality . . . thieves . . . the greedy . . . drunkards . . . revilers . . . swindlers'. However, Paul then makes the most astounding comment: 'And such were some of you. But you were washed, you were sanctified, you were justified in the name of the Lord Jesus Christ and by the Spirit of our God.' The 'saints' are those who were sinners but who are now saved by grace. Why would you not return to the Lord and to the smile of his favour?

Have you not concealed your transgression for too long? (see *Prov.* 28:13). Have you not harboured the notion that your rebellion and breaking of God's law are too much for the grace of God to pardon? Such thoughts detract from God's mercy and detract from the redeeming work of his Son. These thoughts keep you at a distance from the God of all grace. Think of David. Then re-enact his prayer for mercy.

27

GOD'S CHASTENING OF DAVID BEGUN

2 Samuel 13

David's sin against God began as a sexual dalliance with Bathsheba. It proceeded to the murder of her husband. The God of justice forgave David's sin and lifted the sentence of death from his head. Yet the Almighty declared, 'Now therefore the sword shall never depart from your house, because you have despised me' (*2 Sam.* 12:10). He also decreed that the women of David's house would publicly suffer sexual abuse (*2 Sam.* 2:11). What David had unjustly done to Uriah would return upon his own head to the end of his days.

Amnon was David's eldest son. Amnon 'loved' Tamar, his half-sister, David's daughter (*2 Sam.* 13:1). Because she was 'beautiful' she was at the centre of his constant dream. His first thought each morning was of the fair princess. Royal protocol kept her at a distance from him. So Amnon pined and withered away from 'lovesickness' (*2 Sam.* 13:2). The burning flame of 'affection' was consuming him by using his own being as fuel. He poetically thought of her eyes and hair, her beautiful form, and gracious movements. His desire was for the warmth of her embrace. He felt he could not live without having this sweet thing; so he would break with social custom and risk even the throne to have her.

Every ingredient of the popular love song was here. Every titbit of the classic love novel or television soap opera was in his heart. But we will hold Amnon in contempt and will feel deep pity for Tamar at the end of the story. Amnon's romantic fairy tale was not true love.

1. Infatuation Is Not Love

Amnon was infatuated with Tamar. He was strongly attracted to her beauty and charm. These fascinated him and captivated his mind. His feelings were stirred to the depths. Infatuation is a very all-consuming experience which many mistake for love.

2. Amnon Did Not Love Tamar, Because He Did Not Know Her

Because he was a distant admirer of Tamar, Amnon could not really love her (*2 Sam.* 13:2). His view of her was fed by imagination, not reality. Amnon and Tamar had a cousin named Jonadab whose leading feature was the shrewdness of a fox (*2 Sam.* 13:3). Having persuaded Amnon to confide in him as to what was troubling his spirit, Jonadab played on and expanded his cousin's sexual fantasy. One can hear him saying, 'Imagine yourself alone in your bedroom with Tamar . . . Let me tell you how to bring her there' (*2 Sam.* 13:5). With all the cleverness of modern pornographers and the writers of suggestive literature, Jonadab enhanced Amnon's desire to use Tamar for self-gratification.

Amnon followed Jonadab's script. He appealed to David to send David's own daughter into his entrapment of her. Who is less suspecting of children's wiles than are parents? Whose sympathies are more ready to cater to their every wish? Amnon did not love Tamar. He could not, for his attention was exclusively fixed on selfish sexual pleasure.

Even when alone with her in his apartment Amnon never saw the real Tamar. Her physical beauty blinded him to her finer qualities. She was a member of a royal family, but she was not averse to common work such as baking bread. She was also obedient to her father and willing to serve the sick. Then, when confronted with her brother's vile intention to rape her she argued with him: 'No, my brother, do not violate me, for such a thing is not done in Israel; do not do this outrageous thing' (*2 Sam.* 13:12).

Tamar had a spiritual depth that enabled her to understand that Israel was holy to the Lord. She knew that sex outside of marriage was a disgrace and beneath the servants of the Most High God. She further argued that the act would bring shame to her, and it would make Amnon look like a fool. Such acts in secret are bound to become known. Tamar was a realist with high ethical standards (*2 Sam.* 13:13). Although Amnon's crude advances must have been repulsive to her, Tamar did not even rule out an appropriate relationship between them.

'Please speak to the king, for he will not withhold me from you', was her cry.

But it was all in vain. Furthermore, no sooner did Amnon have his way with Tamar than he hated her! (*2 Sam.* 13:15). At once his hatred for Tamar was stronger than his 'love' had been. She had burst the bubble of his dream. Tamar did not melt into his arms: she resisted him. The encounter had not played out as he and Jonadab had conjured up in the fantasy.

Now he had some real idea of who Tamar was. She was not the girl of his dreams, fulfilling his every appetite without question. In Tamar there was much more than physical beauty to admire. She was a woman of depth and substance. Yet Amnon had no inner weight with which to appreciate her deeper beauty.

Therefore Amnon sent Tamar away (*2 Sam.* 13:15). 'No, my brother,' she responded, 'for this wrong in sending me away is greater than the other that you did to me.' She thus argued that they should work through together the long-term consequences of their sexual union. There were responsibilities to be faced. How quickly and tragically today do sexual partners and even counsellors suggest that these partners have no obligations to one another! As David had learned with Bathsheba, although their affair should never have taken place, once it had done so there were practical implications. There were duties toward each other and toward society at large.

But Amnon had his servants eject poor Tamar and bolt the door behind her. In his heart he had washed his hands of her.

3. Sexual Intimacy Outside of Marriage Harms One's Partner

Sexual intimacy outside of marriage exposes one's partner to grief; therefore it cannot be an act of true love. We are given a word-picture of Tamar walking from Amnon's apartment in utter desolation. She was filled with a bitter sense of a life-changing calamity having befallen her (*2 Sam.* 13:19-20). Love 'does not insist on its own way' (*1 Cor.* 13:5) as Amnon had done. Love sacrificially gives itself for the honour and wellbeing of a wife, as did Jesus for the church (*Eph.* 5:25-26). How many are emotionally and really desolate due to pre-marital sex!

Sexual intimacy outside of marriage also exposes one's partner to danger. This episode of history continued for two years, during which a silent Absalom (Tamar's full brother) plotted the death of Amnon. As Jonadab would later tell David, the murder of Amnon by Absalom had 'been determined from the day he violated his sister Tamar' (*2 Sam.* 13:32). David's adultery eventually led to the murder of Uriah. Amnon's rape of his half-sister led to his own murder. Thus even those who were innocent in these situations were drawn into their very ugly consequences.

What kind of person would spill the blood of someone because of extra-marital sex? Ask policemen who work in our large cities. Apart from murders connected with the drugs trade, the most common cause of murder is sexual entanglement. Satan's lie is that the man and the woman are independent. What they do in private is no one else's business. But women have fathers and husbands and brothers. Proverbs 6:26–35 warns, 'A married woman hunts down a precious life. Can a man carry fire next to his chest and his clothes not be burned? Or can one walk on hot coals and his feet not be scorched? So is he who goes in to his neighbour's wife; none who touches her will go unpunished ... For jealousy makes a man furious, and he will not spare when he takes revenge. He will accept no compensation; he will refuse though you multiply gifts.'

4. David's Failure in the Family

David was an effective administrator of his kingdom. However, throughout these connected incidents of rape and murder he was an ineffective father within his family. 'When King David heard of all these things (between Amnon and Tamar), he was very angry' (*2 Sam.* 13:21). But there is no evidence that he called Amnon to account. Perhaps, because Absalom said nothing about Tamar to Amnon for two years, David thought that the matter would heal itself. When Absalom murdered Amnon and fled, we only read that 'the spirit of the king longed to go out to Absalom, because he was comforted about Amnon, since he was dead' (*2 Sam.* 13:39). Later, when Adonijah sought to usurp David's throne, we are told, 'His father had never at any time displeased him by asking, "Why have you done thus and so?"' (*1 Kings* 1:6). Through his neglect in the discipline of his children the sword came upon his household by the hands of these same children.

Sadly, David's sons manipulated him, drawing him into their foul deeds, which broke his heart. We have already seen that Amnon succeeded in seducing Tamar by having David send her to his apartment. Later Absalom enlisted David's aid in sending Amnon to the scene of his murder (*2 Sam*. 13:24–27). Still later, Absalom would play on his father's emotions so as to be invited back to Jerusalem where he intended to slay his father and become king. Ahijah would do as he pleased, never expecting his father to question his actions. David's gullibility in the face of his children's actions seemed boundless.

5. Enduring Chastening

The sexual abuse of David's daughter by her half-brother occasioned the drawing of a sword against the royal household. It produced the chief, but not the only one who wielded that sword. From that day warfare among the sons of his various wives was in their hearts. Even Solomon would have to use the sword against the family to secure his throne. Little do Christians think of the far-reaching consequences of their sins, even when these sins are pardoned!

The 'prince of the power of the air' has a special set of arguments to blind Christians. As he leads a believer to sin, the prince hides the fact that intentional breaking of God's law after having received grace through Jesus Christ is a despising of the Almighty (*2 Sam*. 12:10). Perhaps even the grace of God received at conversion is misused by this prince of darkness.

Some of our sins in the days of our ignorance and unbelief deserved severe temporal and after-this-life punishments. Yet, when the love of God our Saviour appeared to us in the tender mercies of Christ, many of us were so pardoned that we did not experience the expected consequences of our sins. With pardon and the breaking of sin's dominion came also deliverance from many of the just deserts of sin. With almost a note of surprise the Apostle Paul spoke of mercy toward his pre-Christian sins because of his ignorant unbelief (*1 Tim.* 1:13). To the believer the Serpent whispers, 'Why not sin now that God loves you? Surely the Lord will withhold the usual fallout of sin as he did before!'

When the recipient of the abundant pardon of God sins against the loving kindnesses of the Father, the Son, and the Spirit, he not only despises God's holy laws, but also his sovereign grace. Therefore, often must the believer who returns to brazen sin limp for the remainder of his days under chastening sorrows. At the incident of Bathsheba and Uriah there is drawn a line in David's life. The segment across that line is filled for David with many bitter experiences.

Still, Christians who have despised the Lord to plunge into some great sin after experiencing so much of God's pardoning grace must not despair. When David humbly confessed his sin, God quickly announced his pardon. It is possible to live in the sweet assurance of sin forgiven even after a great relapse. But usually the re-pardoned saint will not return to the halcyon days of the springtime of love with God. Chastisements continue, even with the fresh assurances of forgiveness and eternal life.

For any who dwell in this condition there is a special word of assurance:

For the Lord disciplines the one he loves,
and chastises every son whom he receives.
It is for discipline that you have to endure.
God is treating you as sons (*Heb.* 12:6-7).

If anyone who reads this is a person who once delighted in God's grace but now is far from that sunlight, let him not imagine that all great sins of despising God prove that one's former religious experiences were hypocritical. David was no Saul, although his despising of God seems similar to that of the former king. Peter was no Judas, although he was unfaithful to Christ.

Return again and look into the face of Christ. He will ask, '*Do* you love me?' You will have to answer. And you may hear the Saviour say that when you are old, it will not be as it was when you were younger (*John* 21:15–19). Yet Peter was not cast off by our Lord when he turned from his sin in bitter anguish of soul, determined to follow him all the rest of his days.

28

BETRAYED!

2 Samuel 13–15

Through the incidents of Amnon's rape of Tamar and Absalom's murder of Amnon, disgrace and the sword had come to David's household. However, there was yet another strand of the predictive prophecy of Nathan which David was about to experience. The Lord had said through his prophet, 'Behold, I will raise up evil against you out of your own house' (*2 Sam.* 12:11).

1. We Are Always Unprepared for Betrayals

None of us is ever prepared for our nearest of kin, our most beloved, our most trusted friends to become our enemies. We cannot walk through life holding every companion under suspicion. Confidence is placed in those who have shared years of common pursuits and have suffered through common trials. Trust is deepened as mutual loyalty is displayed by serving in a shared cause.

If we have showered devotion on a family member or leaned heavily in reliance upon a friend it is unimaginable that he will be the one to betray us. He may lay a snare for us before our very eyes, and we will explain away the evil intent. We are not suspicious when a plot of his devising is in plain view.

For this reason David did not recognize the most obvious sedition of his son Absalom nor the duplicity and treason of members of his inner circle of government. The sudden bewilderment he felt when the web of evil was fully woven added to the intensity of pain which he experienced.

2. The Hardening of Absalom

After he had murdered his brother Amnon, Absalom fled to a Syrian district in the mountains east of the Sea of Galilee, where he remained for three years (*2 Sam.* 13:38). Far from calling his son to account for the bloodshed, King David affectionately yearned to see his son (*2 Sam.* 13:39).

In the tradition of all flatterers David's nephew and senior military commander, Joab, used his nearness to David to discover the deepest desire of the ruler's heart. Then he pretended to love what David loved: Absalom. Time would show that Joab had absolutely no fondness for Absalom. The general would end the life of David's son against the express instructions of the king. But, for now, Joab would feed David's longing after his own son in order to gain some advantage from the King of Israel.

Through his devious flattery Joab brought Absalom back to Jerusalem from his exile of three years. Nonetheless, David did stipulate that Absalom would not be permitted to 'come into my presence' (*2 Sam.* 14:24). Ungrateful for Joab's earlier services and wishing to have the ban lifted which kept him from the presence of his father, Absalom set fire to Joab's barley crop in order to get his attention. Having had one crime go unpunished, there formed within Absalom a brazen and violent spirit.

His intention was that Joab would plead for the ending of the two-year ban from Absalom's seeing the face of the king. Once more Joab's mediation secured what was really also the desire of David's heart. His beloved son Absalom humbled himself before David. The king gave him a kiss of reconciliation (*2 Sam.* 14:33). For David there were sincere emotions toward his son. For Absalom, as we learn from subsequent events, there was no reciprocal affection for his father.

3. The Rebellion

Access to David was required for Absalom to enact the next stage of his ambitious intrigue. He purchased horses and chariots, and hired fifty footmen to run before his extravagant equipage. He determined that he would daily make this impressive appearance on the road leading to the gate of the city, the place where trials were held and official transactions were made. This plan was put into place and acted upon with great success.

Before those with lawsuits came to the 'court' of Jerusalem, Absalom would discuss their cases with them. He would tell each person that his was a good cause. Then he would belittle David for having appointed an insufficient number of elders or judges to hear cases. He would add that, were he a judge, everyone would receive justice! When grateful citizens sought to bow before the king's son, a flamboyant and handsome Absalom would embrace and kiss them. 'So Absalom stole the hearts of the men of Israel' (*2 Sam.* 15:6).

4. The Coup d'Etat

After spending a few more years of systematic captivation of the hearts of the people, Absalom asked David for permission to go to Hebron. Taking God's name in vain, he falsely reported that his purpose was to fulfil a vow to the Lord. However, Hebron was the city in which David was at first crowned as king. Absalom was in reality planning for his own coronation.

Spies were sent throughout all the tribes of Israel. By trumpet sound a signal was to be passed along from city to city. At the sound of the trumpet the spies would announce in each place, 'Absalom is king at Hebron!' (*2 Sam.* 15:10). The plotting son of David had invited two hundred men from Jerusalem to go with him to Hebron. Furthermore he summoned David's trusted advisor, Ahithophel. Numerous men of Israel responded to the announced coronation and gathered at Hebron in support of him.

Finally word reached David that, 'The hearts of the men of Israel have gone after Absalom' (*2 Sam.* 15:13). David gave the orders to his remaining faithful band, 'Arise, and let us flee, or else there will be no escape for us from Absalom. Go quickly, lest he overtake us quickly and bring down ruin on us and strike the city with the edge of the sword' (*2 Sam.* 15:13-15). His own son sought to kill him. Ahithophel was among the conspirators.

5. David's Anguish

Psalm 41 was composed by David from the inner torments of this betrayal.

> All who hate me whisper together about me;
> they imagine the worst for me.
> They say, 'A deadly thing is poured out on him;
> he will not rise again from where he lies.'
> Even my close friend in whom I trusted,
> who ate my bread, has lifted his heel against me.
> But you, O LORD, be gracious to me,
> and raise me up, that I may repay them!
> (*Psa.* 41:7–10).

To be the object of contempt and of predicted disaster is a stinging spiritual injury. But to have a trusted friend who lived upon your generosity engage in scheming for your downfall is the greatest shock and sharpest heartache. We translate 'the man of my peace' as 'close friend'. Someone with whom he was at peace designed his ruin. The one 'who ate my bread', who enjoyed my hospitality and fed on my generosity, joined those who conspired against me. Such experiences shake our confidence in other men and in our own judgment of who is trustworthy. Absalom! Ahithophel!

It is strange that David's experience was to prefigure, to some extent, our Saviour's own sufferings. David was receiving stripes for his own despising of God. Jesus, who was 'holy, innocent, unstained, separated from sinners' (*Heb.* 7:26), although personally undeserving of enduring such grief, had the iniquity of us all laid on him (*Isa.* 53:6). In experiencing the treason of Judas, the Substitute 'carried our sorrows' (*Isa.* 53:4). John 13:18 quotes Psalm 41:9 as predictive of Christ's experience. Judas' hurtful betrayal 'fulfilled' this text.

Our Lord was not surprised by Judas' treachery as we are stunned when trusted friends join our enemies against us. Frequently the Gospels witness to Jesus' omniscience by showing us that throughout their relationship the Messiah knew which disciple would betray him. For him there would be no moment of uncomprehending shock. Yet the injury of unrequited love to Jesus' heart was nonetheless deep and genuine.

Up to the very moment that Judas valued his Teacher's life at thirty pieces of silver, Jesus heaped kindness on the traitor. Judas was chosen by Christ to be included among his special twelve. Judas was given no less attention and inclusion in the special band than were others of the apostles.

On the very night of betrayal Jesus washed Judas' feet. Jesus, at their last meal, handed to Judas a piece of bread dipped in wine sauce, a gesture of offered friendship. These symbols of Jesus' friendship to Judas were not staged acts of pretence. His heart of love was behind them. At the blackest moment of Judas' betrayal (as he spoke the word, 'Rabbi', and gave his identifying kiss), even then was Jesus not insincere in responding to Judas, 'Friend, do what you came to do' (*Matt.* 26:50). Christ felt the affection of friendship toward Judas even as Judas despised that endearment.

For Christians the most unexpected evil is betrayal from within the church of Christ. We expect unfaithfulness from the world. But it is mind-boggling when brothers and sisters join a conspiracy against us or are the initiators of injustice. When those who break heavenly manna with us are disloyal, it has a devastating impact. It may be very disillusioning.

We must remember that our Saviour was betrayed by an apostle. Even church leaders from the purest (earthly) churches may be unfaithful to the sheep. It is not some strange thing that happens to us (*1 Pet.* 4:12) in these circumstances. Let us not stumble and fall over such fiery trials. Paul could write of his experiences in the church of Christ, 'At my first defence no one came to stand by me, but all deserted me ... But the Lord stood by me' (*2 Tim.* 4:16–17).

Let us learn to stand by the saints. We must pray for the grace of steadfastness and loyalty within the body, lest we be stumbling stones to Christ's sheep when they are under assault.

> The sufferings of the church, like those of her Redeemer, generally begin at home: her open enemies can do her no harm, until her pretended friends have delivered her into their hands; and, unnatural as it may seem, they who have waxed fat upon her bounty are sometimes the first to 'lift the heel' against her.
>
> BISHOP HORNE

29

DAVID'S MOURNFUL RETREAT

2 Samuel 15:13–17:29

It was reported to David that the nation of Israel had turned its allegiance to Absalom (*2 Sam.* 15:13). In response the king ordered a hasty flight from Jerusalem for his family and servants. He wished to deliver those loyal to him from the sword and to spare Jerusalem from an armed assault by Absalom's forces (*2 Sam.* 15:14). There was a large minority who remained loyal to David. At the very outset his servants asserted, 'Behold, your servants are ready to do whatever my lord the king decides' (*2 Sam.* 15:15).

A Philistine who had long served as a military officer with him said, 'As the LORD lives, and as my lord the king lives, wherever my lord the king shall be, whether for death or for life, there also will your servant be' (*2 Sam.* 15:21). All were not turncoats. It must have been comforting in his hour of weakness to have many men display patriotism and loyalty. These traits are too rare in most ages, but, where found, they shine with brilliance.

Still, the exodus from Jerusalem was conducted with a bearing of humiliation and sorrow. The caravan would descend the slope from Jerusalem, cross the Brook Kidron, ascend the Mount of Olives, and then proceed through the northern desert of Judah to the fords of the Jordan River.

The growing multitude of loyalists would there await news of Absalom's intent to pursue. All the while they were poised to cross the river into Trans-Jordan and to proceed to Mahanaim where they would build their defences.

David himself made the journey to the top of the Mount of Olives walking barefoot and with his head covered, which were signs of humble sorrow. Those who attended the king made similar displays of mortification, adding to them abundant tears. Perhaps Bathsheba and Solomon were found in this woeful retinue. There was no boasting, nothing of proud display.

Even as David gathered his servants (including his personal bodyguard contingent composed of the Cherethites and the Pelethites) to begin the doleful march, Zadok, Abiathar, and the priests who were bearing the ark of the covenant arrived to pledge their allegiance and to go with David. The king sent these spiritual leaders back into Jerusalem. They were instructed to be David's eyes and ears in Absalom's capital. Any significant intelligence of Absalom's intent to pursue David could be carried to their leader by the hands of Ahimaaz, Zadok's son, and Jonathan, Abiathar's son. David would wait at the fords of the Jordan for any news.

As the hours passed, the priests sent word by their sons to David of Absalom's mobilization for war. The young men barely escaped with their lives as they fulfilled the king's request (*2 Sam.* 17:15–22). Their faithfulness delivered all of the king's loyalists from danger.

Part of the way up the Mount of Olives, a messenger arrived to tell David, 'Ahithophel is among the conspirators with Absalom' (*2 Sam.* 15:31). Ahithophel was a man full of wisdom who had been one of David's most intimate and most trusted advisors. If some were loyal, some were treacherous. Upon hearing this news, David immediately turned to his God in prayer: 'O LORD, please turn the counsel of Ahithophel into foolishness' (*2 Sam.* 15:31).

When David reached the top of the Mount of Olives he worshipped God at a location where God's people often went for their devotional exercises. In disgrace and under chastisement David expressed his full and undying homage to the Lord of hosts. Do you continue to worship in the low moments of your life, or do doubts suspend your prayers until brighter times arise?

At this place Hushai, a close friend of David and another trusted counsellor, caught up with the king. He came with torn robe and with dust upon his head, grieving over the misfortune of his friend. Because Hushai was aged, David said, 'If you go on with me, you will be a burden to me' (*2 Sam.* 15:33).

David asked his friend to return to Jerusalem, to feign allegiance to Absalom, and to be the means God would use to turn Ahithophel's counsel into foolishness. Though he was of a great age, he was asked to infiltrate the enemy camp to its innermost circle and to be David's secret envoy. At least David could tell Hushai that Zadok and Abiathar would be his allies.

If David was stung by Ahithophel's treason, he must have sensed the sweetness of having hearty counsel with this friend Hushai (*Prov.* 27:9). Ahithophel's treachery cannot be too strongly condemned. Scripture insists, 'Do not forsake your friend and your father's friend' (*Prov.* 27:10). Job reminded his three friends when they turned against him, 'He who withholds kindness from a friend forsakes the fear of the Almighty' (*Job* 6:14; the ESV rendering here is very close to John Calvin's in his *Sermons on Job*).

It was eventually the Lord who undermined Ahithophel's advice to strike David before he had protection or an adequate hiding place. 'For the LORD had ordained to defeat the good counsel of Ahithophel' (*2 Sam.* 17:14). Therefore everyone preferred Hushai's advice, which was to wait until overwhelming force could be assembled. Word was sent to David through the priests to waste no time in leaving the region of the Jordan (*2 Sam.* 17:1–16). Ahithophel was probably wise enough to realize that the acceptance of Hushai's advice doomed Absalom and would lead to his own eventual death. Thus he committed suicide (*2 Sam.* 17:23). But David was not helpless even in flight.

Just as David and his entourage were entering the desert region, Ziba approached the king. Ziba was the former servant of Saul whom David had appointed to manage the lands of Saul for Mephibosheth's benefit. To David and his household he brought a gift of bread, raisins, summer fruit, and wine, to refresh them on their journey (*2 Sam.* 16:1–4). When David enquired about Mephibosheth, Ziba slandered the son of Jonathan, claiming that the recipient of David's kindness was hoping to inherit David's throne.

His words are neither established nor denied by Scripture, but they do not ring true for many reasons. Rather, it seems that Absalom's treason was infectious, turning other servants against their masters. Ziba was using David's weakness for personal advantage. In this he appeared to succeed, as for a time David gave the fruits of Saul's lands to Ziba as a return for his kindness.

Soon after his encounter with Ziba, David passed through Bahurim, a village on the way to Jericho. Shimei, who was of Saul's family, lived there. Hearing that the son of Jesse was in disgrace and was travelling through his neighbourhood, Shimei followed the king's caravan for some distance. He shouted curses at David, kicked up dust, and pelted David and his servants with stones. Shimei continued to do this for some time, notwithstanding the strong men surrounding David to protect him (*2 Sam.* 16:5–13).

Shimei called David a 'man of blood' and a 'worthless man' (*2 Sam.* 16:7). He accused the king of being guilty of all the blood of Saul's house that had been spilled. He claimed that the Lord had given the kingdom to Absalom as vengeance for David's wicked actions against Saul.

Abishai, David's nephew, and the brother of Joab, asked, 'Why should this dead dog curse my lord the king? Let me go over and take off his head' (*2 Sam.* 16:9).

There is something right about Abishai's comments, something that is right in every age and every nation. Too many in western democracies overlook Romans 13:1–2: 'Let every person be subject to the governing authorities. For there is no authority except from God, and those that exist have been instituted by God. Therefore whoever resists the authorities resists what God has appointed, and those who resist will incur judgment.'

Peter (*2 Pet.* 2:9–12) describes the 'unrighteous' as those who 'despise authority. Bold and wilful, they do not tremble as they blaspheme the glorious ones [or dignitaries, NKJV], whereas angels, though greater in might and power, do not pronounce a blasphemous judgment against them before the Lord.' Shameful accusations are made by ordinary citizens and by the news media against our rulers in modern times. Such speech is a sin, destructive of authority and order in society. It is against the will of God.

Jude also denounces 'people' who, 'relying on their dreams, defile the flesh, reject authority, and blaspheme the glorious ones' (*Jude* 8). In addition Jude reminds us that, since the devil was given a certain authority by God, Michael the Archangel when 'contending with the devil . . . did not presume to pronounce a blasphemous judgment [against the devil]' (*Jude* 9). However, these dreamers 'blaspheme all that they do not understand' (*Jude* 10). How easy it is to use immoderate language to denounce public officials about matters we do not understand! The sin of Shimei has filled the political landscape and news broadcasts of the West.

Shimei and modern evil-speakers against dignitaries are pathetic figures. They are bitter in spirit for the misfortunes they have encountered in life. They easily believe theories of conspiracy, thinking that authorities have intentionally injured them. They seethe inwardly, willing to draw conclusions without evidence.

They read God's providence in their own selfish and misguided interests. They triumph over other men's tragedies. They have never listened to Proverbs 24:17, 'Do not rejoice when your enemy falls . . .' David's reply, while suffering such impudence, indicates the frame of heart which controlled him throughout his grief-stricken journey. David looked beyond the false charges of this man. Behind the cursing of Shimei was the providence of God! It was the Lord who had brought this man to curse him.

All of the king's attention would not be to the accuser; he would give far more consideration to the Lord who had arranged this event. It was David's thought that if he patiently endured this providence in the fear of God, perhaps the Lord would have mercy on him (*2 Sam.* 16:10–12). Besides, 'My own son seeks my life.' Compared with this disaster, what are a few curses from the Benjamite?

Surely David recalled his own sins against Uriah and Bathsheba. He was innocent of Shimei's accusations. Yet his heart was humbled with the sense of genuine sin that had brought God's curses upon his household. Thus he behaved himself with self-effacement, casting himself on the mercy of God. In similar fashion, when we face false accusations, we should remember our true sins, sins of which our accusers may be totally ignorant.

The lesson for us, then, is one of submission to God's providence, because we know all too well that our enemies might hurl true accusations if they but knew all there is to know about us. This they could do if they had God's knowledge of our hearts or even our own powers of self-examination.

Suffering unjustly, with hearts contrite before God, may draw his pity; he might even arise to deliver us. David's expressions of humiliation were not a mere external display. They were the products of a heart which was truly sorry for sin and was looking to God for assistance. How easy it is to assault a stranger who brings bitter words while overlooking the greater crime of a child with murder in his heart. Let us learn from God's grace in David to suffer well under unmerited attacks, knowing that the Almighty may bring them upon us as a providential rebuke for sins of which we are guilty. This fear of God in our hearts may please him and bring much longed-for relief.

Let us also remember our Saviour, who deserved none of the abuse that he suffered in this world. How patiently he endured the vile assaults upon him, knowing that God in justice was laying upon him the iniquity of us all! Meditation on the purpose of God in bringing us to grief is more conducive to having that grief end than is attacking the human instruments who trouble us.

When David arrived at Mahanaim, again he was greeted by loyal patriots. Shobi, Machir, and Barzillai did what they could to comfort the company of David, showering their own wealth on the hungry and weary travellers (*2 Sam.* 17:27–29). These men had lived through earlier days when raiders were spoiling their goods in Trans-Jordan. At that time David had defeated their enemies, thus enabling them to accumulate wealth. They were grateful for a ruler who did for them as God intended he should. In David's hour of need, therefore, they showed their gratitude with voluntary support of their champion's cause.

30

CIVIL WAR ONCE MORE

2 Samuel 18:1–19:8

There was only one battle between Absalom and David. Absalom directed the attack against his father. He had a much larger force in the field, which he placed under the command of Amasa. David divided his smaller defensive forces into thirds, appointing Joab, Abishai (Joab's brother), and Ittai the Gittite as captains. The two forces engaged in combat on the east side of the Jordan River in a wooded area.

Absalom's army suffered the death of twenty thousand men in a day, and Absalom himself was killed. The soldiers loyal to him then fled, realizing that their attempt to overthrow David was doomed and that they might well go the way of Absalom. The first casualty of the battle actually had been the very wise man Ahithophel. As we have seen, when Absalom refused to conduct the war as he had advised and chose instead a scheme which could not succeed, Ahithophel took his own life.

1. History's Lessons

When we visit famous battlefields we often observe monuments. Children are especially fond of those monuments which realistically represent the scene of history. There may be a statue of a hero in battle attire astride a mighty horse. Or there may be carved panels picturing opposing forces rushing toward one another with drawn swords. From these we receive an idea of the excitement and fearfulness of a war which has long ago passed into history.

Bible history is filled with picturesque monuments from ancient times. Absalom is carved into the Bible in hideous scenes to impress upon us all that God was serious in commanding:

> 'Honour your father and mother' (this is the first commandment with a promise), 'that it may go well with you and that you may live long in the land' (*Eph.* 6:2–3).

Absalom, on the contrary, was active in attempting to end his father's life. He had assembled a mighty army for the purpose of destroying his father. As a consequence, God cut off Absalom's life on the earth before he had lived very long. It did not go well with Absalom. Thus we see that God has made Absalom a monument by which one can understand this foundational moral principle of life.

At the foot of this monument is an inscription. It is either, 'If one curses his father or his mother, his lamp will be put out in utter darkness' (*Prov.* 20:20), or it is, 'The eye that mocks a father and scorns to obey a mother will be picked out by the ravens of the valley and eaten by the vultures' (*Prov.* 30:17). The monument itself has two sides.

One side depicts a very handsome Absalom whose head is caught in an oak tree, his feet helplessly hanging above ground level. Approaching him are Joab, carrying three sharp spears, and his armour bearers (young men), who carry swords. These men are about to slay Absalom. On the other side of the monument is displayed a pit in the forest upon the top of which we see a heap of stones.

Absalom had decided that David, his own father, must die so that he could take the king's throne. For years this faithless son had plotted to win the favour of the people whom David ruled. He had slandered his father and had boasted that he would rule the kingdom more wisely (*2 Sam.* 15:1–5). His efforts to turn the nation against his father had succeeded so well that most able men in Israel actually did volunteer to help Absalom fight against their king.

We must remember the Scripture which says, 'Though the wicked sprout like grass and all evildoers flourish, they are doomed to destruction forever' (*Psa.* 92:7), and, 'He who is often reproved, yet stiffens his neck, will suddenly be broken beyond healing. He who . . . hardens his neck will suddenly be destroyed and that without remedy' (*Prov.* 29:1, NKJV).

As Absalom's scheme came together, he led a huge army into combat against David's lesser numbers. David's place of exile had been clearly identified.

2. God's Attention to Every Detail

However, God caused the battle to turn against Absalom's forces. As already mentioned, twenty thousand of his mighty warriors were slaughtered (*2 Sam.* 18:7). In order to escape from the troops of David, Absalom himself fled, riding a mule. His mount ran swiftly under the thick branches of the forest. At the direction of the Almighty, Absalom's head was jammed into the branches of an oak, as the mule ran out from under him.

Joab and his men executed Absalom, for God made Joab think that the death of David's son would make his army lose heart. Following that a trumpet was blown to disengage the armies, so that no further slaughter of fellow-countrymen would occur. *Kingdoms are given and withheld by the Lord.* 'For there is no authority except from God, and those that exist have been instituted by God' (*Rom.* 13:1). Absalom, who was so vain in his life, came to a shabby end. He was without a proper burial and without any honours at his death. His body was unceremoniously hurled into a pit in the woods, and rocks were cast over that body until it was covered.

3. Graves and Memories

What a contrast there is between this memory of Absalom and the one he had planned for himself! Having no son to carry on his name, he had erected a pillar in his own honour in 'the King's Valley' (*2 Sam.* 18:18). No doubt this refers to the valley between the Temple Mount in Jerusalem and the Mount of Olives. There, kings and prophets were buried.

In our day one can still find, in the Kidron Valley, 'The Tomb of Absalom'. The present structure so named dates from many years after Absalom shamefully perished with his arm raised against his own father. Scripture does not tell us if David's family had the remains of Absalom removed from the pit and buried near the pillar which Absalom had built. Nor do we know if 'The Tomb of Absalom' is built upon the exact site of that pillar.

4. Sorrow for the Dead

As the one battle was being staged, David had publicly charged his captains, 'Deal gently for my sake with the young man Absalom' (*2 Sam.* 18:5). It was no surprise, therefore, that when the two messengers brought David tidings of the battle, his one concern was to ask, 'Is it well with the young man Absalom?' (*2 Sam.* 18:29, 32). When the second messenger responded, 'May the enemies of my lord the king and all who rise up against you for evil be like that young man' (*2 Sam.* 18:32), 'the king was deeply moved.'

For some time the overwhelmed father cried, 'O my son Absalom, my son, my son Absalom! Would I had died instead of you, O Absalom, my son, my son!' (*2 Sam.* 18:33). Never was it more evidently displayed that war may be almost as tragic to the victor as to the vanquished.

David's worst fears before the combat had now become dark reality. Death had swallowed another of David's sons. His first son by Bathsheba and his son Amnon had preceded Absalom in death. Having experienced the grave's swallowing of one's children does not ease the anguish of a new incident of this affliction.

An object of the father's love was painfully and permanently snatched away from earthly fellowship. In such an hour, there floods into a parent's heart a felt awareness of the vanity and the deplorable brevity of life since the Fall. Despite all of Absalom's faults, David loved him still.

Worse still, death had seized Absalom without his ever having expressed a word of regret or repentance for his many crimes against his father and other family members. Any gesture of remorse might have eliminated the sting of his contempt for and rebellion against David. How many have injured family members and then have hastened to their tombs with never an apology to diminish the pain of the one who is left! The survivor is bereaved of one whom he loved dearly, yet one who remained at enmity with him.

However, the sharpest ache in David's heart arose from his full awareness that Absalom had hastened away to the judgment of Almighty God. His death came because of rebellion against his parents.

A sudden destruction. A violent assault. A shameful disposal of his body in a pit. Infamy. Disgrace. The hand of the Lord had seized a hardened sinner, and that sinner was his own son.

It is a strange contradiction of life that our faith leads both to exalted joys and to precipitous sorrows. Being informed by Scripture that the wicked shall be cast into hell but the righteous shall never perish has two consequences for the believer. The first is that he feels jubilant gratitude for a Saviour who delivers from the deserved curses of the Most High. Yet the same beliefs intensify our misery when someone we love goes away to judgment, leaving us with no reason to believe that he has found God's mercy in Christ. The wicked will spin dreams of pleasant things awaiting those like themselves after death. The saint cannot indulge in such delusions without denying the essence of his faith. He must suffer a peculiar agony when a wicked family member dies. He suffers this because he loves righteousness and hates iniquity; he was taught to do so by the Lord Jesus. But the one who has died in his sins has never listened to the gospel with faith.

5. High Costs of Prominence

Sometimes we imagine that to gain popularity and to rise to prominent leadership are things greatly to be desired. Yet often the eminent can find no place to hide from public view. Their pre-eminence exacts a fee of embarrassment in those delicate moments when they are overwhelmed with misfortune and grief. Celebrities are denied private hours to weep and to recover composure. In just this manner all of David's sorrow for Absalom, even his excessive sadness, was observed and noted by many.

There was no time to indulge his sorrow. Men had risked their lives against an army of overwhelming proportions to deliver their ruler from grave danger. Brave patriots and loyalists required David's attention, commendation, and thanks. An evil, bloodthirsty, vain, traitorous rebel must not have his sympathies, even if it was his son.

Joab, who had dispatched Absalom, spoke to David roughly with arguments and threatenings to awaken the king from his over-indulgence of compassion for Absalom. Brought to his senses by the shocking rebuke of Joab, David saluted the victorious band who had restored the kingdom to him.

We see another example of this necessity much earlier in Israel's history when Aaron and his sons were conducting worship in the tabernacle (*Lev.* 10:1-7). Aaron's two sons, Nadab and Abihu, 'offered unauthorized fire before the LORD, which he had not commanded them' or stipulated for his worship (*Lev.* 10:1). As a consequence, 'fire came out from before the LORD and consumed them' (*Lev.* 10:2). Moses ordered some Levites to carry the bodies of Nadab and Abihu out of the sanctuary. However, Aaron and his two other sons were commanded not to react to this traumatic double death in the family with ordinary expressions of mourning. They had higher responsibilities, to conduct tabernacle worship for the whole congregation.

It is clear from these Scriptures that excessive indulgence of grief over the death of the wicked may interfere with higher obligations in the service of God. All that we do is before the eyes of the Ruler of all providence. We must not provoke the Lord with intemperate outpourings of emotion as though we are fundamentally disapproving of divine justice.

God had many years before called David 'a man after his own heart' (*1 Sam.* 13:14). This surely did not mean that David would not sin nor take mistaken steps. Yet when he went astray he humbled himself before the Lord and his prophets, repenting and returning to the ways of the Lord. With all God's chastening of his servant, God was still making a house and an everlasting throne for David. The kingdom shook. Then it was returned to David's grasp.

31

AN ELDERLY MAN OFFERS NOBLE SERVICE

2 Samuel 19:32–40

When the rebellion had been subdued, the victorious king retraced his route of flight. As he travelled from Mahanaim to Jerusalem, people far and wide recognized that David's re-crossing of the Jordan River would be symbolic of triumph and of the joyful restitution of his reign. That scene is described in great detail in 2 Samuel. At the fords of the Jordan a multitude met David. We are given a vivid picture of the events that occurred.

There was Shimei who had brazenly cursed David as he left Jerusalem. As David approached this grand moment, Shimei with equal brazenness cried out with abject pleas for pardon. David cautiously spared his life.

Then came Ziba and Mephibosheth, who sounded in the king's ear conflicting accounts of a dispute between them, each hoping to secure the ruler's favour. David's meeting with Mephibosheth was accompanied by tense conversation. The king asked Jonathan's son why he had not gone into hiding with him. When he had been fleeing from Jerusalem, David had heard Ziba's account of Mephibosheth's absence. Only upon his return did the lame man have opportunity to give David his account of that event. His assertions were two: First, Ziba had disobeyed his orders and had taken advantage of his disability to leave Mephibosheth stranded in Jerusalem. Secondly, Ziba had slandered Jonathan's son in David's hearing.

Thus two men who pledged loyalty to David had conflicting accounts. The facts lay hidden between the contending parties. Seasoned judges have no access to hearts to observe who is speaking truth and who falsehood. It should not surprise us that even wise men cannot get to the bottom of personal quarrels. David ordered the two men, Ziba and Mephibosheth, to share equally in Saul's estate. Having no further information, even-handedness was the best that he could do.

God knows whether Ziba slandered Mephibosheth in order to steal half of his estate or whether Mephibosheth cleverly lied his way out of blame for thankless behaviour toward the king. Scripture does not clearly vindicate or assign guilt to either man. At times there is no satisfying justice in human courts. Yet God knows all and will set all things right in the last day. Slander is a serious offence in God's eyes.

In addition various leaders of Judah and Israel assembled there to argue with one another in David's presence, each one hoping to gain political advantage. In the midst of these sharp discordant noises, Sheba initiated another armed insurgence before the very face of the monarch. There would be swift bloodshed to end this rebellion lest, as David said, 'Sheba . . . do us more harm than Absalom' (*2 Sam.* 20:6).

1. Quiet Dignity

While the tumult of strife and the clamour made by individuals seeking personal assistance increased in penetrating volume, David's eye was attracted to a more quiet company of mounted men. These men had no political agenda to argue and no favours to request. At their head was the familiar face of an octogenarian. It was Barzillai who had only become known to the king a short time before. He, his family and his friends had heaped food and comforts upon the king and his household-in-exile.

David had met this gentleman in an hour of need and had been the recipient of his generous charity, freely offered. Now, at the Jordan, he had come once more to give to David. Barzillai, his sons and perhaps his grandsons sat in silent dignity observing the return of the kingdom to David. They had travelled to this important event to salute the Champion of Israel. They had come to give honour to their sovereign as he rode in power and majesty toward his palaces.

Do we not often approach assemblies of the Son of David our King, Jesus? How many seek advantages there! If needs are great our Lord's grace and power are such that he can meet them all. Others, perhaps not sensing great need, nonetheless draw near in hopes of increasing a party and identifying it with the Saviour. How few approach consciously longing only to give unto the Lord at God's right hand all glory and honour and blessing. Should we not come to offer first our hearts and then our praises? It is thus that we may enjoy the Lord's presence and his advancing kingdom.

David singled out of the swirling masses the elderly Barzillai. A royal invitation was given: 'Come over with me, and I will provide for you with me in Jerusalem' (*2 Sam.* 19:33). Barzillai was personally chosen by David to be his honour-guard from the Jordan to Jerusalem, and then to be his guest so long as he pleased.

2. The Psychology of the Elderly

In their brief discussion on horseback Barzillai told the king of his condition, which is the common experience of most who reach the neighbourhood of four-score years in age. For younger acquaintances of the elderly, there is a need to understand that these among us may not be made to act and feel young again.

For Barzillai the ability to enjoy sensual pleasures was greatly diminished. 'Can I discern what is pleasant and what is not? Can your servant taste what he eats or what he drinks? Can I still listen to the voice of singing men and singing women?' (*2 Sam.* 19:35). This does not mean that there are no satisfying pleasures for the elderly. 'Though our outer nature is wasting away, our inner nature is being renewed day by day' (*2 Cor.* 4:16). While the sensual strengths fade, spiritual powers and enjoyments may be increased. But it is no use recruiting the elderly for youthful parties or palatial feasts.

It should not have surprised David that Barzillai would feel out of place in the festivities of the king's court. The gates of his senses no longer opened wide to material delights. The hinges were rusted. Yet Barzillai did not hold in contempt the good things which the young can enjoy. Not despising the king's offer, he asked that his son (or grandson) Chimham replace him in experiencing the offered privilege.

Also Barzillai felt that he was a burden to others. 'Why then should your servant be an added burden to my lord the king?' (*2 Sam.* 19:35). How could Barzillai, eighty years old, keep pace with the king in riding? Yes, he would cross the Jordan as David's honour-guard. But then he would turn back so as not to impede the king's ascent to Jerusalem. This feeling that others are held back in order to include the elderly is not a misimpression. The aged who are still keen of mind know that their stride keeps others from travelling at the rate which they would enjoy.

Barzillai illustrates that the godly elderly are thinking about and preparing for death. Nothing is as unbecoming to the elderly as to put the subject out of mind. 'How many years have I still to live? ... Please let your servant return, that I may die in my own city near the grave of my father and my mother' (*2 Sam.* 19:34, 37).

Most would like to die at their own homes where there are peculiar comforts and familiar surroundings. They have chosen a place of burial. The young should not be disturbed by this combination of thoughts.

3. The Usefulness of the Elderly

Barzillai was not just folding his hands and waiting to die. There was still much that he was doing and that he could do exceedingly well. If he was slow in riding horses, he was as quick as anyone to leap at an opportunity for benevolent acts toward the saints. How he comforted David and his family in their distress!

If there was honour to be given to his king, Barzillai would be at the head of his clan. He was still leading his family. He was instructing his sons and grandsons in dignified behaviour in the presence of rulers. Would the younger heads of his house have entered the political arguments at the Jordan if the patriarch had not been there? Would they have kept their sights on the most important issue of the moment without his example? It was not a day to secure things for themselves but to give support to the king in his glory.

> 'The righteous flourish like the palm tree and grow like a cedar in Lebanon. They are planted in the house of the LORD; they flourish in the courts of our God. They still bear fruit in old age' (*Psa.* 92:12–14).

Although elderly children of God can recall having had greater powers in youth, and thus they do not 'feel' themselves to be 'fresh and flourishing', yet to God and to other men there is appreciation of their vintage services. If there is a day left on earth, it may be used to lay up treasure in heaven.

In David's eyes Barzillai's contribution was the *crème de la crème* of faithfulness to a ruler. David rode by his side across the Jordan. Then 'the king kissed Barzillai and blessed him, and he returned to his own home' (east of the Jordan, *2 Sam.* 19:39).

Even so does our Lord Jesus cherish the service of his loyal, elderly servants. Of their faithful attendance on their Lord's worship and of their giving to the needy in his name, Christ takes note. Of their enduring to the end in family duties and community service, Christ is tenderly appreciative.

Even godly thought of dying is for the Lord. 'If we live, we live to the Lord, and if we die, we die to the Lord' (*Rom.* 14:8). We do not die to satisfy some strange desire in ourselves. We are ready to die if it be his will. That too will be for him. Perhaps in crossing the Jordan of death the Lord himself will ride beside us.

4. The Earthly Reward of the Elderly

The depth of David's appreciation for Barzillai was shown in actions toward his son Chimham. In just the same way David had been showing his love for Jonathan in his treatment of Mephibosheth. When Barzillai turned back 'to his own home', 'The king went on to Gilgal, and Chimham went on with him' (*2 Sam.* 19:40). What greater blessing can our Lord give us than to accept our children in his service when we are too weak to go on!

The account in Samuel closes as David and Chimham ride into Gilgal together. There is little doubt that Chimham continued on to Jerusalem, there to enjoy the delights of the king's court that had been offered to his father. Perhaps David even took Chimham under his wing as something of a replacement for the lost affection of Absalom. It is within the realm of possibility that Chimham would have been granted a portion of David's personal estate as well.

Four hundred years later, in Jeremiah 41:17, we read of 'the habitation of Chimham, which is near Bethlehem' (NKJV). What blessings fall to later generations through the continued steadfastness of the elderly!

We all feel a special love for Zechariah and Elizabeth, for Simeon, and for Anna. When younger generations had forgotten to look for the Messiah, elderly saints gave masterful service to him. So may elderly saints always be cherished and useful in all the churches of Christ.

32

THE TERROR OF THE LORD

2 Samuel 21:1–14

David's life was unendingly encumbered with the household of Saul. While Saul lived, David was always hiding himself in secret places or was banished from his homeland. When Saul was slain in combat with the Philistines, Judah crowned David king. Yet for ten years David was in an armed stand-off with Abner, Saul's first cousin who controlled the ten tribes of Israel through manipulation of Ish-bosheth (Saul's son). While fleeing for his life from his own son Absalom, David endured the slanders, curses, and violence of Shimei who was 'of the house of Saul'.

As victory over Absalom was being savoured, the king again had an unpleasant confrontation with Shimei and was compelled to settle a squabble between Mephibosheth (Saul's grandson) and Ziba (Saul's servant). No sooner were these annoying matters settled than Sheba, of the tribe of Saul, instituted a new rebellion against David by the ten tribes of Israel.

All of this occurred before David had set foot in Jerusalem following the civil war. Finally, on the last day of his reign David found it necessary to instruct Solomon on the handling of Shimei (*1 Kings* 2:8-9).

Other fallout from the misdeeds of Saul required the attention of David in his administration of the kingdom. A sample of these knotty problems is given to us in 2 Samuel 21:1–14. This incident began without David's awareness that Saul had had anything to do with a current serious difficulty in his nation. There was famine in Israel for three consecutive years (*2 Sam.* 21:1).

1. The Fear of God before Created Powers

If rains were withheld and harvests failed to appear, David's thoughts turned to the Lord our Maker. Rains do not come and go by materialistic determination, nor are they influenced only by lesser causes. The courses of sun, moon and stars, the tides, winds, rain clouds and seasons were created by God and continue to be directed by his providential government. Famine is not a consequence of material forces alone. Even these come by the will of God, as do floods, hurricanes, volcanic eruptions and all 'destructive' forces. Being a God of infinite power as well as of infinite wisdom, the Lord has reasons why nations are afflicted by these calamities. Thus 'David sought the face of the LORD' as to why the God of Israel had brought this to pass (*2 Sam.* 21:1).

Through prophetic offices at his disposal David requested an explanation from the Most High. The Lord's administration is over the affairs of earthly governments.

It is instructive to note that David could not discern God's reason for bringing famine on Israel. He could no doubt identify many evils among the people of Israel which might deserve such a response. However, it required divine revelation to specify what had provoked God's anger in this instance. In our times, some Christian ministers have taken it upon themselves to explain precisely what factor was on God's mind in his bringing about a natural tragedy or a military catastrophe. Yet these men are not prophets. David, being a true prophet, waited for the Almighty to explain himself.

God does visit the furies of created powers upon nations because of their moral guilt. Ruinous earthquakes, floods, winds, and drought should lead us to repentance for all of our sins, but we must be cautious not to claim knowledge of the particular sin which lies behind a particular desolation.

2. The Fear of God at the Awareness of His Omniscience

By bringing famine on Israel God was avenging a national policy enacted decades earlier by a ruler long-since silent in the grave. Saul had sought to exterminate the Gibeonites from Israel. When Israel had entered Canaan under Joshua's leadership centuries before David lived, God had commanded his chosen nation to exterminate the Canaanite tribes. They were to make no treaties of peace with any who had preceded them as inhabitants of the land. The Gibeonites by elaborate deceit (*Josh.* 9) had persuaded Joshua and the elders of Israel to swear by the Lord God of Israel not to harm them.

For numerous generations the Gibeonites had been integrated into Jewish life in Israel. However, Saul began systematically to put these people to death. Perhaps his motive was to seize their lands and to give their property to others in order to secure loyalty to his authority from the recipients of his gifts (this pattern in Saul's thinking is disclosed in *1 Sam.* 22:7). But, whatever Saul's reasoning had been, this was an offence to the Lord, by whose name Israel had sworn not to harm the Gibeonites.

As years passed Saul's outrageous crime against God and the Gibeonites faded from most minds. All of us have a tendency to tremble as we are doing evil. We think such things as: 'What If God were to see and to expose my crime to others? What if the Almighty so directs that just punishment swiftly falls on me for this misdeed?' Sadly, if the just vengeance does not immediately overtake us, these impressions recede.

We forget. We think time will heal the wrong done. The current news holds our attention and suppresses our recall of our own past acts of shame. But God's thoughts are not like our thoughts. His omniscience does not dim, nor is his remembrance confused by the passage of time. The joining of perfect recall with infinite holiness and justice should make us all quake before our Judge. In this instance we see that after many years God sent famine to Israel for Saul's national sin (*2 Sam.* 21:1).

3. Fear before the God of Holy Wrath

David summoned the Gibeonite elders. He knew that the Jews must 'make atonement' to the Gibeonites (*2 Sam.*

21:3). The king asked the injured party what would 'cover' the injustice done to them. A ransom price must be paid. They must agree upon a substitute gift whose worth would cancel Israel's debt to these people. This is the Old Testament language of expiation. It would be used in the New Testament for 'the Lamb of God who takes away the sin of the world' (*John* 1:29). The offering of the infinitely worthy blood of the Son of God will cover over or cancel the debts of all sins before God. 'You were ransomed ... not with perishable things such as silver or gold, but with the precious blood of Christ, like that of a lamb without blemish or spot' (*1 Pet.* 1:18-19).

As David negotiated a *kopher* (ransom price) for social redemption with the Gibeonite leaders, it was revealed that through the years these men had come to understand Moses' law better than had Saul. David asked, 'What shall I do for you? And how shall I make atonement, that you may bless the heritage of the LORD?' (*2 Sam.* 21:3). The Gibeonites declined monetary payments. Jewish law forbade receiving money to expiate bloodshed (*Num.* 35:31). Only the shedding of blood would atone for murder. The Gibeonites did not wish that just any Israelites should suffer capital punishment. They therefore asked that seven descendants of Saul be given over to this sentence, because there had been the slaughter of their forebears.

David complied. Seven descendants of Saul were slain by the Gibeonites who 'hanged them on the mountain before the LORD' in Gibeah of Saul (*2 Sam.* 21:6). Ordinarily the body of an executed man was buried before sunset. These remained exposed until 'God responded to the plea for the land' in sending rain. Both the Gibeonites and the God of heaven and earth were appeased by this redemption price. The sin of Saul and of Israel was thus covered by vengeance upon a substitute.

4. Scripture and the Gospel Call Us to Fear God

From grisly scenes such as this one we learn what God means by the revelation of himself in which he says, 'Vengeance is mine, and recompense, for the time when their foot shall slip; for the day of their calamity is at hand, and their doom comes swiftly' (*Deut.* 32:35). As Jesus later emphasized, 'Fear him who can destroy both soul and body in hell' (*Matt.* 10:28).

The Judge of all the earth will not acquit the guilty. Why do men imagine that in the day of the Lord the Righteous and Just One will turn a blind eye toward any sin? Only if a sinner confesses his guilt and brings in his hand a ransom price to cover or atone for his sins will God forgive him. Guilty men who refuse the *kopher*, the substitute payment provided by God himself, will surely fall under his wrath and curse. The Lamb of God has been proclaimed and the price of his blood offered to all who will come to Jesus. What folly it is in man that causes him to scorn that perfect offering!

Western society pretends to be above such ideas as blood payment for great sins. To cater to the delicate tastes of modern man, teaching on the need for blood atonement and appeasement of the wrath of God is set aside. Much is said of mercy, love, and pardon, while a curtain is drawn to hide the transactions by means of which God forgives. The process by which the guilty may be pardoned is unmentioned. Nevertheless, the Bible is not so fastidious.

Is it possible to know the grace of God without having first experienced the terror of God? Paul said, 'Knowing therefore, the terror of the Lord, we persuade men' (*2 Cor.* 5:11, NKJV). Isaiah, whose call to ministry came out of a scene of terror (*Isa.* 6), declared that God would dwell with the one who 'is humble and contrite in spirit and trembles at my word' (*Isa.* 66:2). Moses too was called to preach by God's voice in the burning bush. When God began to speak, 'Moses trembled and did not dare to look' (*Acts* 7:32). A minister's task is not to scrub his message clean of all elements that may disturb his hearers, but to speak with a mind that recalls the fear of God.

After all, our gospel message calls men to 'serve the LORD with fear, and rejoice with trembling' (*Psa.* 2:11). Our hearers are to 'work out [their] own salvation with fear and trembling' (*Phil.* 2:12). Perhaps the absence of 'fear and trembling' in our worship impedes sanctification and perseverance.

At Jesus' birth 'fear fell upon' Zacharias (*Luke* 1:12), and also the shepherds 'were filled with fear' (*Luke* 2:9). At his resurrection 'for fear of him the guards trembled and became like dead men' (*Matt.* 28:4), and even the disciples 'departed quickly from the tomb with fear and great joy (*Matt.* 28:8). Crowds were filled with awe or fear when Jesus healed the paralysed man (*Luke* 5:26); fear came upon all when he raised the son of the widow of Nain from the dead (*Luke* 7:16); they were seized with great fear (*Luke* 8:37) when the Gadarene had the demons cast out of him. These experiences were more than 'loving respect'. They are described for us as visceral responses to a prodigious presence. The nearness of the Most High creates in us uneasiness and apprehension. An inner disquiet and outward trembling are not inappropriate when the Lord draws near. Through the ages men have felt such apprehensions when seeing closely the raw power of thunderstorms (instrumental in the conversions of Augustine and Luther). Others have felt this way in the presence of Almighty power in the life of Christ. Still others have known such tremblings through the preaching of God's Word or in worship (*Acts* 4:31; 24:25).

Old Testament poets have captured this fear of God. David does so in Psalm 29, his thunderstorm Psalm. So does the writer of Psalm 97:

> The LORD reigns, let the earth rejoice; let the many coastlands be glad! Clouds and thick darkness are all around him; righteousness and justice are the foundation of his throne. Fire goes before him and burns up his adversaries all around. His lightnings light up the world; the earth sees and trembles. The mountains melt like wax before the LORD, before the Lord of all the earth. The heavens proclaim his righteousness, and all the peoples see his glory.
>
> PSALM 97:1–6.

33

PREPARATIONS FOR SOLOMON'S TEMPLE

2 Samuel 24

Following Absalom's *coup* and David's restoration to the throne, the aging monarch spent much time on a project close to his heart. God had told David that he, a man of bloodshed, might not build a temple to the Most High. However, his son Solomon would be privileged to erect the house of worship for Jehovah at Jerusalem. Thus David could assemble wealth and building supplies for Solomon's coming venture. Many of the king's latter days were happily filled with these preparations. Administrators were instructed to be ready to assist Solomon with all their hearts and with all their might. The Lord must have a suitable abode.

1. The Sovereign Purposes of God

2 Samuel 24 begins with a measure of disclosure of the mind of God at that time. Although we are told something of God's thinking, his decrees are clothed in clouds of mystery. There are many strands to the

Almighty's purposes folded together with connections which we cannot understand. We are here again reminded of the Lord's words through Isaiah: 'For my thoughts are not your thoughts, neither are your ways my ways' (*Isa.* 55:8). 'No one can find out the work that God does from beginning to end' (*Eccles.* 3:11, NKJV).

It is explained that the incident of 2 Samuel 24 occurred because 'the anger of the LORD was kindled against Israel' (*2 Sam.* 24:1). Because of this anger against Israel's citizens, the living God 'incited David against them'. That is, God set in motion events that would cause David to sin, to make a serious mistake in the governance of Israel. In response to David's sin the Almighty sent a destroying angel to punish the nation by slaying 'of the people from Dan to Beersheba seventy thousand men' (*2 Sam.* 24:15). As David later appeased the wrath of God against his sin, he declared of the place in which he made the sacrifice, 'Here shall be the house of the LORD God and here the altar of burnt offering for Israel' (*1 Chron.* 22:1).

God was angry because of the sins of Israel. Yet, God intended to designate the place at which his temple should be built for the people of Israel. God led David to sin so as to bring wrath upon Israel and to bring appeasement for their (the people's and David's) sins at the future site of the temple. Justice and mercy are mysteriously mixed in God's predestination and in his carrying out of his purposes.

Many will be disturbed to read that 'the LORD . . . incited David' to sinful action (*2 Sam.* 24:1). Yet all the Scripture witnesses to the fact that all evil acts of men have as their ultimate cause the decree of God. Moses told Pharaoh that the Lord had said, 'for this purpose I have raised you up, to show you my power, so that my name may be proclaimed in all the earth' (*Exod.* 9:16). The early church prayed, 'In this city there were gathered together against your holy servant Jesus, whom you anointed, both Herod and Pontius Pilate, along with the Gentiles and the peoples of Israel, to do whatever your hand and your plan had predestined to take place' (*Acts* 4:27–28). Scripture routinely teaches that God's sovereign purposes are guiding all sinful acts of men.

Although 2 Samuel 24:1 asserts that the Lord incited David to his sin, 1 Chronicles 21:1 tells us that Satan incited David to this same sin. These are not contradictory accounts. God's moving was the ultimate or first cause; Satan's moving was the secondary or instrumental cause. When God determines that men should act righteously, he sends the Holy Spirit directly to move them to righteousness. 'It is God who works in you, both to will and to work for his good pleasure' (*Phil.* 2:13). However, when men act wickedly it would be blasphemous to say that it is God who works in them. To the contrary, 'The prince of the power of the air' is 'the spirit that is now at work in the sons of disobedience' (*Eph.* 2:2).

If fallen men are to please God, his Spirit must implant the grace to be righteous, directly moving them to good works. If evil acts of men will serve God's will, all that is needed to produce sin is already in their hearts, and Satan is standing by, eager to stir it up. All God need do is withhold his mighty restraint of evil and allow it to run its course, so far as it suits his purposes. It was godly Augustine who referred to God's 'efficacious permission' of evil. Although he is not the author of sin, the Holy God directs sin to his intended ends. His plan is equally ultimate in bringing about righteousness and sin. Yet, these two purposes are *not* brought to pass 'in the same way' (another Augustinian phrase).

When we have said all of this, we are not pretending to comprehend the mind of God; we are seeking to express it, as far as revelation permits. We continue to fear and wonder before God's inscrutable wisdom and supremacy.

2. The Sin

That which Israel did to arouse God's anger is not specifically mentioned. Throughout their history, from their sojourn in Egypt to the time of David's reign, there were serious departures from God in one form of idolatry or another. Then there were Israel's two rebellions against the Lord's anointed one, under Absalom and under Sheba. The Scripture does not specify what provoked the Lord and brought about this particular judgment.

In David's case we do know that the sin was numbering the fighting men in Israel and Judah. Perhaps a tendency in older men was stirred in David's heart by Satan. In later years some count their wealth. Others count their military forces. Their accounting feeds pride and self-confidence. It is a short step for such a one to trust in the arm of flesh or to glory in riches. All the while his confidence is not being placed in the Lord to protect him from emergencies which might arise. Did Satan tempt David to look away from the Lord to his own resources? Or did Satan bring reports of military threats which prompted the numbering?

People who are subject to national leaders scrutinize the decisions of those who make national policy. Much self-righteousness stands behind the assigning of blame to rulers for each misdeed or miscalculation, whereas all the while failures and corruption in princes may be brought to the surface because God is angry with the populace at large. This was the case with regard to David's corrupt act.

Holy Scripture records numerous sins by older saints whose service to God in younger years was greatly blessed. It is a sad reminder that we may not expect to make progress into temptation-free territory in this life. Remaining sin and Satanic devices must be fought rigorously to the very end. Moses was sinfully angry at a very advanced age. Noah fell into shameful drunkenness after he righteously stood against an unbelieving world for many a long year. David was not out of the Devil's reach when his hair was grey. Perfectionism is a myth till death or Christ's coming overtakes us.

3. The Sincere Repentance of David

When Joab's officers returned to David with the census of men capable of military service David's conscience smote him. This time he needed no prophet to say, 'You are the man!' (*2 Sam.* 12:7). 'And David said to the LORD, "I have sinned greatly in what I have done. But now, O

LORD, please take away the iniquity of your servant, for I have done very foolishly"' (*2 Sam*. 24:10).

David's grace and godliness never shone more brightly than in his statements of contrition for sin and his pleas for pardon. There is no question that the Lord specially loved David. This is not because David had no scandalous sins. Rather, it is because he was always broken and penitent for his sins.

It is important to note that God's chastisements of David always fell upon him *after* he had humbly repented. Only after David had admitted to God and to men, 'I have sinned against the Lord' in the affair with Bathsheba, were any chastisements experienced. It was afterwards that his firstborn to Bathsheba died and family tragedies ensued. In the case we are now considering, David repented. The very next morning, Gad the prophet arrived to announce God's intention to smite Israel.

David was asked to choose between three expressions of God's displeasure. He replied, 'I am in great distress. Let us fall into the hand of the LORD, for his mercy is great; but let me not fall into the hand of man' (*2 Sam*. 24:14). When you have sinned do you firmly believe in the mercy of God in Christ and prefer God's visitation rather than that of man? Have you not found men more cruel than the Lord?

Just as the destroying work of God's angel had fallen upon all the kingdom from Dan to Beersheba, even so the avenging messenger of the Lord of hosts stood prepared to smite Jerusalem. Seeing this angel, 'David spoke to the LORD . . . and said, "Behold, I have sinned, and I have done wickedly. But these sheep, what have they done? Please let your hand be against me and against my father's house"' (*2 Sam.* 24:17). Even in his humiliation David exhibited a shepherd's heart. His great psalms and moving prayers came from hours such as these.

4. The Selected Place

It was in Salem (Jerusalem) that Abraham had met Melchizedek, the priest of the Most High God, the prefigure of Messianic priesthood. Later God would take Abraham back to Mount Moriah, on the outskirts of Salem, to offer up Isaac his son. There a substitute for Isaac was provided and offered to God in his stead. Now, at this crisis in David's life, the avenging angel of the Lord stretched out his hand over Jerusalem from this same mount, just outside Davidic Jerusalem.

Gad instructed David to erect an altar to the Lord on the threshing floor of Araunah the Jebusite on Mount Moriah. David purchased from Araunah the threshing floor along with oxen to sacrifice. David there offered burnt offerings and peace offerings. 'So the LORD responded to the plea for the land, and the plague was averted from Israel' (*2 Sam.* 24:25). This spot would become the house of the Lord and the altar of burnt offering for Israel (*1 Chron.* 22:1).

How appropriate, yet how mysterious, that the Temple Mount should be purchased in an hour when the people of Israel desperately needed their sins propitiated, when Israel would either perish or have the wrath of God against their sins turned aside! The religion pictured at the temple was not one designed for righteous men, offering up their good works to God. The temple depicted sinners under the wrath and curse of God finding a sacrifice to which to transfer their guilt and God's displeasure against them. The urgent need to be cleansed of sin and to escape God's vengeance leads inevitably to a sacrificial lamb.

It was at this Jerusalem, a thousand years later, that the Lamb of God was sacrificed to take away the sin of the world. For a millennium the temple sacrifices pointed to his coming. 'He has appeared once for all at the end of the ages to put away sin by the sacrifice of himself . . . offered once to bear the sins of many' (*Heb.* 9:26, 28).

After Christ's sacrifice, which truly and finally removed sin for all who call upon him in faith, there was no need of temple shadows. The real sacrifice had taken place. In AD 70 the temple and its figurative sacrifices were removed. The religion of peace with God for sinners through the appeasement of the just anger of God by a holy Sacrifice is now declared the world over.

The temple rose amidst a sinning nation with a sinful king to declare that there was coming a living way to God for all sinners. This becomes so much clearer in the light of the New Testament revelation of the Son of God.

34

A FINAL MESSIANIC PSALM

2 Samuel 23:1–7

Throughout the latter years of his reign, David was looking to the future. He prepared his administration to support Solomon in building the great temple for the Lord. He accumulated funds and building materials for this project which was first born in his heart. Even in the dire plague to avenge David's last recorded sin of numbering the fighting men of Israel and Judah, the king acquired and devoted the threshing floor of Araunah as the future site of the temple.

In addition David contemplated the terms of God's great covenant with him. Especially did the promises of that covenant brighten his last days with hope for the future. We too, all who are recipients of the glorious promises of the New Covenant in Christ, should meditate upon the exquisite hope that awaits us in the coming kingdom. It is too easy to close out our days sinking into a bog of regrets for sins of which we long ago repented, or enumerating the pains and weaknesses which intensify and accumulate in greater number as we age. Our eyes should be lifted up to a delectable future highlighted by the promises of God.

The writer of Samuel prefaces David's last psalm with, 'Now these are the last words of David' (*2 Sam.* 23:1). Some have taken the words to be David's advice to Solomon. That is not the case. The words are clearly a Psalm. The 'Ruler over men' is the Messiah. The kingdom described is the reign of the Messiah over all the earth. Nonetheless, any inferior ruler, reigning over a less extensive kingdom, would do well to imitate the Lord Jesus in character and policy.

1. The Psalmist Appears in His Own Song

'The oracle of David, the son of Jesse, the oracle of the man who was raised on high, the anointed of the God of Jacob, the sweet psalmist of Israel' (*2 Sam.* 23:1b). This is not the first time that David began a Messianic psalm by reflecting on himself at the start of his poem. He did so in Psalm 45:1. Psalm 110 begins with the Lord speaking to David's Lord.

Though he is a prophetic observer, David is inserted into the psalm in which Christ is all the glory. He will always be the son of Jesse and part of the astounding family whose genealogy runs backward through the book of Ruth to Abraham. He is also 'the man who was raised on high'. Though of little note in the eyes of his family when he was assigned keeper of the sheep, God raised David up to be King of Judah and Israel and to be the most notable ancestor of Jesus Christ since Abraham (*Matt.* 1:1). It was the one true and living God who anointed David to be king and prophet. Jesse's son was conscious of having composed praises to God which would be as sweet smelling incense before the Almighty's throne: 'For it is good to sing praises to our God; for it is pleasant, and a song of praise is fitting' (*Psa.* 147:1). The psalms are sweet to God and sweet to the servants of God.

David also expressed his consciousness of being a vessel in which the Lord had revealed his truth to the children of men: 'The Spirit of the LORD speaks by me; his word is on my tongue. The God of Israel has spoken; the Rock of Israel has said to me' (*2 Sam.* 23:2–3a).

God the Holy Spirit carried David along (*2 Pet.* 1:21) as God breathed out his words (*2 Tim.* 3:16). These words were placed on David's tongue so that David could claim, 'Thus says the LORD', the God of Israel. The Rock of Israel spoke to the anointed one, and the anointed one in turn delivered the very words of God to his fellow-men. This was not a natural process, to David's mind.

2. The King is Overshadowed by the King of kings

The theme of David's last psalm was the noblest and sweetest subject of composition. We must remember that it is not David speaking to Solomon. It is the Rock of Israel speaking to David. The sweet psalmist of Israel is given a glimpse of:

> A Ruler over men, who is just,
> A Ruler in the fear of God (*2 Sam.* 23:3b).

There will arise a descendant of David, a Ruler, not merely of Israel and Judah, but over all mankind. The inspired psalmist here became a seer of the coming Christ, the Ruler whose dominion dwarfs all other thrones. We have sold all to purchase an interest in this Ruler, if we are his followers. His preciousness is beyond calculation. Tell us all that the God of Israel said of Jesus!

All authority in heaven and on earth has been given to him (*Matt.* 28:18). 'But we see . . . Jesus, crowned with glory and honour' (*Heb.* 2:9). 'For he must reign until he has put all his enemies under his feet' (*1 Cor.* 15:25). 'A Ruler over men': 'The kingdom of the world has become the kingdom of our Lord and of his Christ, and he shall reign forever and ever' (*Rev.* 11:15). In former psalms David had spoken of Christ's resurrection when the Father would say to him: 'Ask of me, and I will make the nations your heritage, and the ends of the earth your possession' (*Psa.* 2:8).

He had described the Ascension of Christ, as the Saviour would return triumphantly to the throne room of heaven (*Psa.* 110). He had described Christ's return to earth for his bride, the church (*Psa.* 45). Now we see his last words; they are of Christ's eternal reign, which will be fully established at his second coming.

Messiah's character and rule will be 'just'. This Hebrew word, often used in the Old Testament, is translated into English both by the word 'righteous' and the word 'just'. A person or government which adheres strictly to the moral law of God is both righteous and just in all their ways. In saying this we must remember that the chief component required for obeying every command of God is love to the Lord as well as love to neighbours.

What are the most common complaints against every government over men? First, there is the criticism of corruption. Widespread selling of favours and governmental powers for personal enrichment by those in authority drains away actual service to *all* men. Secondly, the office holders and government agencies become impersonal, insensitive to the needs of those over whom they rule. At times they brutally oppress the righteous, misusing the authority given to them.

In the light of actual failures by rulers with fallen natures, the Old Testament often joins this idea of justice (also righteousness) in rulers with their defending the poor, the infirm, widows, orphans, foreign residents in their nations, and all others who are subject to economic and social oppression.

David clearly saw the shining quality of the coming Christ and his kingdom as justice or righteousness. In this the kingdom of God and its king would stand out in sharp contrast with all who had gone before him. Such justice and righteousness arise only from 'the fear of God': 'A Ruler, just, a Ruler in the fear of God.'

No other ruler ever had such an intimate relationship with God the Father as did Jesus Christ. He *always* acted to please the Father with the fullest loving devotion during his first mission on the earth. When he comes again in power and glory to institute the final phase of his eternal kingdom, all will continue to be done in the perfect fear of God. The fear of God is the beginning of wisdom and righteousness for rulers as well as for other citizens of nations.

Jesus' earthly ministry was marked with service to the multitudes, with compassion for the disadvantaged and suffering, and with special attention to the poor. He fed the hearts and bodies of the hungry. He made men whole spiritually and eternally. His moving invitations to all who were weary and heavy laden continue to echo in our memories. In his fear of God, his righteousness and his justice, the Messiah will continue to subordinate his personal interests to those of his sheep. He will forever stand above manipulation by contrary interests. He will be approachable by the most needy under his rule.

3. Dual Consequences of Messiah's Reign over All the Earth

When Christ is elevated upon earth to institute his complete command of all earthly affairs there will be two equally stunning repercussions. 'Every eye will see him' (*Rev.* 1:7), 'when the Lord Jesus is revealed from heaven' (*2 Thess.* 1:7) to set all things right upon earth. To those who have trusted him and are loyal to him: 'He dawns on them like the morning light, like the sun shining forth on a cloudless morning, like rain that makes grass to sprout from the earth' (*2 Sam.* 23:4).

Living under rulers who are not fully just or fully righteous is a dismal existence. Sometimes life is lived in the darkness of night. At other times it is not in pitch blackness that we walk, but still there are dreary clouds looming over us constantly. The coming of Christ will be to his sheep the brilliant sunrise on a morning without clouds or like the refreshing rain on parched ground that carpets the earth with fresh green grass.

'Although my house is not so with God, yet he has made with me an everlasting covenant, ordered in all things and secure. For this is all my salvation and all my desire; will he not make it increase?' (*2 Sam.* 23:5, NKJV). Although David's house and dynasty do not match the justice and righteousness of the coming Ruler, yet by grace God has made with David an everlasting covenant. That covenant, founded on God's pledge, is ordered in all things and secure. God would make David's house increase. From his line the Messiah would come and triumph over all.

This reign of Christ was all David's salvation and all his desire. His hope in his last days remained fixed on God's promises and on the Christ who embodied them. His soul yearned for the fulfilment of all the terms. This is the expectation of all the redeemed, completely centred in the person and reign of Christ. However, when Jesus 'comes on that day to be glorified in his saints, and to be marvelled at among all who have believed' (*2 Thess.* 1:10), on that same day he will inflict 'vengeance on those who do not know God and on those who do not obey the gospel of our Lord Jesus Christ' (*2 Thess.* 1:7-8).

'But worthless men are all like thorns that are thrown away, for they cannot be taken with the hand; but the man who touches them arms himself with iron and the shaft of a spear, and they are utterly consumed with fire' (*2 Sam.* 23:6–7). A Ruler, just and righteous, must destroy the wicked. They are as ungovernable as thorns, painfully piercing the ruler and kingdom that seeks to manage them. Thorns must be dealt with by hard (iron-like) measures, especially by the spear. Fire will suddenly overtake all sons of rebellion against God and his Messiah. They will quickly be consumed where they stand ('in their place', *2 Sam.* 23:7, NKJV). Until Christ comes God has 'instituted' inferior earthly rulers (*Rom.* 13:1–7). Even now their commission from God is to defend and support those who are good and 'to execute wrath on him who practises evil' (*Rom.* 13:4, NKJV). If that is God's expectation, the Messiah will hold accountable to this standard all judges, lawmakers, and government administrators. Their day of judgment before his throne will come. The delight of enjoying newborn grass on a bright morning after rain requires that the thorns, which have no fear of God, and thus are always in rebellion against the good and against God's law, should be consumed.

'A Ruler—just, a Ruler—in the fear of God' must bring these two consequences to pass for each to become genuine. Humanism, which denies the depravity of man and insists that all are 'good' in their own way, has turned truth upside-down. The insincerity of its adherents is displayed in their vigorously defending the 'rights' of the wicked while holding in contempt the people of God. Messiah is about to come and set these things right-side-up again. 'This is all [our] salvation and all [our] desire' (*2 Sam.* 23:5, NKJV). 'Amen. Come, Lord Jesus!' (*Rev.* 22:20). Does not your soul yearn for these double enactments by the Lord Jesus? David's heart did. Are you his brother in the faith, three thousand years later?

35

DAVID PREPARES TO REST WITH HIS FATHERS

1 Kings 1 & 2

It is difficult to comprehend the extraordinary accomplishments of David. He defeated all of Israel's enemies who threatened her peace. He organized the army of Israel, the government of Israel, and the national worship of Israel (*1 Chron.* 22–29). In addition he composed at least eighty Psalms which have served as the heart of the song-book/prayer-book of God's people ever since. The Spirit of God was mightily with him.

1. The Approach of Death

Still, 'death spread to all men because all sinned' (*Rom.* 5:12). Therefore the greatest saints must also come to the country of Beulah (as Bunyan described the believers' last days), where they wait to cross the final river before being admitted through the golden gates into heaven. Then a messenger is sent to each one to bring the King's summons. When the messenger came to David, he 'slept with his fathers and was buried in the city of David' (*1 Kings* 2:10). 'Then he died at a good age, full of days, riches, and honour. And Solomon his son reigned in his place' (*1 Chron*. 29:28). In the first chapter of 1 Kings and the first quarter of chapter 2 we read of David's waiting at that strange river which is both our last enemy and our passage way to glory.

David is described in physical weakness, as unfit to rise from his bed. At this point his appetite for material pleasures was greatly diminished, and his body was in constant discomfort. Yet, in his circumstances we see 2 Corinthians 4:16 illustrated: 'So we do not lose heart. Though our outer nature is wasting away, our inner nature is being renewed day by day.' In his enfeebled condition David's spirit rose to direct the affairs of his family and kingdom and to express great joy and satisfaction in the prospects of Israel under his successor.

2. Another Assault against David's Throne

All was not quiet for David by the riverside. The final case of 'evil against [him] out of [his] own house', sent by the Lord because David had 'utterly scorned the LORD' (*2 Sam*. 12:11, 14), arose in David's very last days. *Never* did the sword depart from David's house (*2 Sam*. 12:10).

Adonijah, David's son by Haggith, 'exalted himself, saying, "I will be king"' (*1 Kings* 1:5). Expecting his father soon to die, Adonijah allied himself to Joab, commander-in-chief of David's army. He drew in Abiathar the priest to make sacrifices at his self-coronation. Much of the king's household was invited to the festivities.

Adonijah was a wilful and ambitious man. He chose to take advantage of his father's frailty in old age to seize power and influence. 1 Kings 1:6 explains part of the cause of the wilful arrogance of David's son. 'His father had never at any time displeased him by asking, "Why have you done thus and so?"' Never in his childhood or youth did David rein in Adonijah's strong and selfish will.

There can be a false tenderness of parents toward their children which abdicates the responsibility to discipline and shape the characters of those whom God has entrusted to them.

A strong will uncorrected and never denied of its desire leads to the destruction of the one in whose heart it dwells. The stronger a child's will, the more necessary it is that parents say 'No' to it. If parents do not govern a son's will, how can he learn to govern it himself? Such persons will come to grief when they contend with the Almighty. 'Whoever spares the rod hates his son, but he who loves him is diligent to discipline him' (*Prov*. 13:24).

Word of this insurrection reached the ears of Nathan the prophet, and Nathan sent Bathsheba to break the news to David. She reminded the king that he had sworn that Solomon would reign after him. Then she remarked, 'Adonijah is king, although you, my lord the king, do not know it ... And now, my lord the king, the eyes of all Israel are on you, to tell them who shall sit on the throne of my lord the king after him' (*1 Kings* 1:18-20). Immediately Nathan the prophet came in to confirm her report.

David instantly dealt with this crisis. Zadok the priest and Nathan the prophet, attended by Benaiah, captain of the king's personal bodyguard, were ordered to mount Solomon on David's own mule and lead him through the streets of Jerusalem to anoint him king at Gihon. There was great rejoicing in the city 'so that the earth was split by their noise' (*1 Kings* 1:40). Then Solomon was set upon David's throne. Thus was the scheme of Adonijah defeated. Note that, 'When the righteous increase, the people rejoice, but when the wicked rule, the people groan' (*Prov.* 29:2).

David entered into this joy, saying, 'Blessed be the LORD, the God of Israel, who has granted someone to sit on my throne this day, my own eyes seeing it' (*1 Kings* 1:48). Some men prefer to die in office, which means that they never have the pleasure of observing the transition wrought by the placement of capable men in positions to carry on in the future a work well begun for the Lord. This, however, was not the case with King David.

3. Guidance for Solomon

In contrast, with almost his last breath David gave wise advice to Solomon. 'When David's time to die drew near, he commanded Solomon his son' (*1 Kings* 2:1). Each word of advice would have been made memorable by David's moving prelude, 'I am about to go the way of all the earth.' Have you been at the bedside of a beloved father as he died? Have you not tucked away in your memory every saying of that occasion? What solemn moments these are! What deep impressions they make! Some, out of fear, believe that they would like to die in their sleep. But what a blessing it is to be conscious and sound of mind to the end, doing good by one's last words!

General Instructions:

1. *'Be strong, and show yourself a man.'* The churches and nations have need of strong men. Decisive and active leadership *must* be given for the well-being of God's institutions on this earth. The glory of God calls for all our strength and for zeal unbounded.

2. *'Keep the charge of the* LORD *your God,* walking in his ways and keeping his statutes, his commandments, his rules, and his testimonies, as it is written in the Law of Moses.' Monarchs have a charge from God for which they will answer on the Day of Judgment. So too has every lesser officer of the kingdoms of the earth. Only by familiarity with the Word of the living God can leaders know his ways, statutes, commandments, rules, and testimonies. The practice of this principle of sound government is becoming increasingly rare upon the earth, even in the most 'Christianized' nations. Yet rulers *must* constantly review God's Word and live in the fear of God to have commendation from him on the last day.

There are great promises connected to ruling well. Obedience to the written Word of God will lead to prosperity 'in all that you do and wherever you turn'. What a bright and broad expectation of blessing exists for those who serve according to God's Word and who keep that Word fresh in their hearts. Therefore this father mentioned the special Davidic promise of an unbroken family dynasty ruling 'If your sons pay close attention to their way, to walk before me in faithfulness with all their heart and with all their soul'. He knew that faithfulness to God alone would stabilize the throne.

Are any national leaders of this generation moved by such promises? Or does everyone support the laying aside of all religion in secular democracies? Here an aged king advised the next ruler to hearken to the Word of God.

Specific Instructions:

After giving these general directions to Solomon, David spoke of three particulars to which his son must attend. Two of the three matters were related to individuals dangerous to the wellbeing of Solomon's throne.

1. *Joab* had been troublesome to David throughout his reign. This valuable military leader was not subject to his king on a number of occasions. In the most recent instance, Joab had joined Adonijah's grasping after power. It was a crime against David's throne and a threat to Solomon. David advised Solomon to see to Joab's execution in a wise manner.

2. There was also *Shimei* of the household of Saul, who had cursed David and displayed a slanderous hatred of the king. Again David advised a wise arrangement by Solomon which would end in Shimei's execution.

Solomon would not have been able to live and reign with proven subversives like Joab and Shimei. Perhaps an older and well-established David could control them; Solomon could not. In order to establish his kingdom, strong seditious men must be faced and eliminated.

Those who despise all confrontation and conflict are not suited to rule. Not everyone can be considered welcome to live in a nation or in the membership of a church. Although the church may not wield the sword, there are effective spiritual disciplines available to be exercised. No organization which has the goal of doing good can succeed if it allows those who would sabotage its goals to snap at the heels of the leadership with impunity.

3. But along with the stiff tasks assigned by father to son there came the delightful assignment of heaping kindness on one family. David had much of great importance to pass on to Solomon for his son's wellbeing and for that of his kingdom. Among the most urgent matters of business was dealing 'loyally with the sons of *Barzillai*'. David did not forget Barzillai's love for his king to his dying day. His gratitude overflowed from his heart so as to drive him to provide greater benefits still to his dear and loyal friend.

Thank God that positions of strength and authority are not all about intrigue and serious measures of just punishment. The throne may show much kindness, and every officer of a kingdom, of an organization or of a church should use his post for the blessing of worthy subjects.

Of course, the latter part of 1 Kings 2 tell of Solomon's implementing of his father's advice. As he did so, God's Word says, 'So the kingdom was established in the hand of Solomon' (*1 Kings* 2:46). Would that we had the wisdom, not only to serve God well in our generation, but also to pass the baton to younger men with such skill as to issue equal blessing to the rising generation as we die!

These are the words spoken by Benaiah to David: 'As the LORD has been with my lord the king, even so may he be with Solomon, and make his throne greater than the throne of my lord King David' (*1 Kings* 1:37). What leader, conscious of his own flaws, will not desire that the rising generation surpass him in wisdom by the Spirit?

However, David had a higher desire. It was expressed in Psalm 17:15: 'As for me, I shall behold your face in righteousness; when I awake, I shall be satisfied with your likeness.'